MONEY
CHIROPRACTIC and YOU

Thoughts and solutions for the most difficult practice questions.

-- For practicing chiropractors only --

For more information:

Tory M. Robson DC
7114 Shady Oak Road
Eden Prairie, MN 55344

1

Dedication

To all the men and women who since 1895
have dedicated their lives to serving humanity
in one of the greatest professions on earth.
Chiropractic.

These are my uncensored thoughts and
unapologetic opinions gained from the real and
often unforgiving world of chiropractic practice
and consulting. For legal or financial questions
always consult the appropriate accountants,
attorneys, and professional advisors.

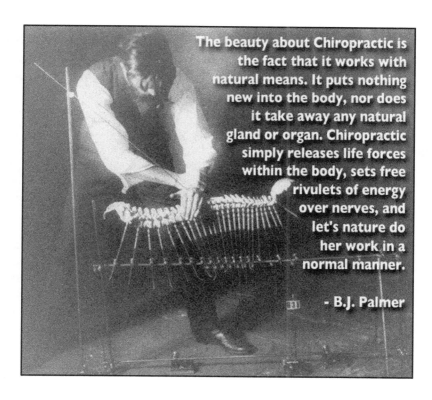

The beauty about Chiropractic is the fact that it works with natural means. It puts nothing new into the body, nor does it take away any natural gland or organ. Chiropractic simply releases life forces within the body, sets free rivulets of energy over nerves, and let's nature do her work in a normal mariner.

- B.J. Palmer

Q: Tory, If You Don't Mind I would Like to Start by Asking You a Few Background and Warm-Up Type Questions.

No sweat, ask whatever you like.

Q: Some Call You a Success Guru, Practice Innovator, the Most Relevant Coach in Chiropractic Today, and Even a Genius Within the Profession. How Do You Respond to This?

Those are kind words. I'm just a regular guy who worked hard and continues to do so. Yes, I have created several new and incredibly useful things for chiropractors. I can only gauge my success from the results of my patients and the success of the chiropractors around the country who have hired me to teach them how to be more successful in practice.

A genius? I don't think so. Nikola Tesla and the amazing architect Frank Lloyd Wright are geniuses. There's a popular quote I like though: *"A genius is someone who understands what is obvious."* What matters to me is the success of those within my sphere of influence. My goal is to be as valuable as I can be to chiropractors and the chiropractic profession.

Q: Fair Enough. So Why Would a Chiropractor Listen to You or Take Advice from You, Especially Compared To All The Other Consultants Out There?

You might find it more interesting to ask my clients this question. As far as other consultants go, I really don't know or care what they do. I am dramatically different from all of them. They have good intentions I'm sure. However, I do wonder how many consultants in chiropractic today are truly qualified. Anyone can call themselves a "coach" and try to sell advice these days.

I created my coaching program because I thought I could offer something better than anything I had seen before. I've personally had over ten consultants and spent over $200,000 on coaching. I learned a lot and I'm very thankful, but I did feel that every program lacked so much. For example: <u>Not once</u> did any consultant I was paying ever ask me how my student loans, debt, or savings were coming along. I thought I hired them to help me be successful?

Money and debt are by far the biggest stressors in the profession today. Not once did any group I was in ever teach me anything useful about handling money. None had any real plan on how to become wealthy in the future from all my hard work. I am still wound up about this and a few other things too, but don't get me started.

I can tell you this, <u>my clients get exactly what they need in the areas that they need it</u>. Floorplan, office systems, scripting, marketing, hiring, staff training, debt elimination, money systems, money management, buying or selling a practice, starting from scratch, wellness plans, getting patients to stay and pay, PI building, insurance maximization, referral generation, website domination, cash practice, PVA building, confidence building, communications skills, de-sissification. You name it, <u>we have it right now, ready to go.</u>

I have my finger on the pulse of chiropractors and the chiropractic profession. I often think of all the chiropractors out there who need help. They are paying for advice, or nodding through another seminar <u>not</u> getting what they really need while I am sitting here with <u>exactly what they do need</u> in audio, video, print, or direct consulting form.

As far as I'm concerned **WINNERSEDGE** has no competition. I actually feel sorry for any chiropractor who is not a member of my group. This is my personal opinion of course.

Now back to your question: Why would a chiropractor listen to me? Here are a few things worth considering:

- I'm now at 22 plus years in successful, active practice and <u>never</u> flatlined, drifted, got bored, or wavered in the mission.

- Though I easily could, I haven't quit and become just another "consultant" who bailed-out, only to then tell you how great practice is and how to be successful at it. I am the real thing and I'm still in the trenches just like you.

- I've had over 25,000 coaching calls with chiropractors and spend another 1500 minutes on the phone with DCs every week. The experience I gain in every conceivable area of practice is enormous. You would not believe what I see and hear.

- I've done Health Talks in over 100+ companies and created and taught 100+ seminars and trainings all over the country. Plus, who knows how many speaking engagements for other seminars, schools, clubs, etc.

- I have now published 32 CD and DVD sets along with over 1000 videos for chiropractors everywhere. Many consider our audio and video materials to be the best in chiropractic today.

- I've designed and personally built myself 6 brand new offices from scratch. In addition, I've designed and overseen the building and money management related to countless more around the country. At any given time I have 5 to 20 offices in different states of construction or re-vamping per my specifications and guidance.

- Every week I consult on practice sales and practice purchases, including all the money planning, transition, and details.

- I've dealt with countless banks, accountants, the IRS, financial institutions, insurance companies, attorneys and the like. I understand how business really works in this country.

- Not to mention the magazine articles I've published. The podcasts, webinars, thousands of hard questions answered and the litany of scenarios I've had to figure out solutions for.

- The lessons continuously learned from the countless money mistakes and money successes I am called to consult on.

- All the information I've gathered from my library of books, videos, and CDs in the study of chiropractic, technique, philosophy, personal success, and how money works in our economy, in our profession, and on a personal level.

- I have bought, sold, leased and been a Landlord for both residential and commercial real estate. Considering the office build-out and subsequent rent are the largest expenses for a chiropractor, experience here is essential. When a doctor client talks to me, they get a serious expert on one of the most expensive things they will ever have to deal with.

- I started from dirt in a town where I knew nobody. I was loaded with serious loans like everyone else and without a free dollar of help from anyone.

- I have personally paid-off hundreds of thousands of debt, using the exact system I teach and began saving religiously with just $100 a month.

- I've collected well over $100,000 per month and over $1,000,000 a year repeatedly in one low overhead office with no associates or anything outside chiropractic. (I feel this is a basic requirement to even be a consultant.)

- I have made more sacrifices than most and still do. I learned from my own successes and mistakes, plus from a few more serious mistakes made by taking the advice of those I never should have listened to. One reason I consult now is to save as many chiropractors as I can from the landmines that await them.

- I have actually done it. I stayed the course and became a net worth millionaire and then a legit cash millionaire. I did so one patient visit at a time without ever deviating from the chiropractic mission, still loving chiropractic, and without destroying everything else in my life including my health.

- I'm near the top of the Chiropractic Mountain, yet the better I do the more I realize how far I can still go. We can all get better.

- Make no mistake about it, I have forged a path that works and now want more chiropractors to follow it. You can trust me when I say that I will lead you right.

Q: This May Be Skipping Ahead, But What Is Your Ultimate Goal for The Chiropractors You Deal With?

Simple. The goal I have for all my chiropractor clients is to change thousands of lives with incredible chiropractic care. As a result they reflect great honor and credit upon themselves, their family, and the chiropractic profession. This goes for all CAs and team members also.

Additionally, using our superior systems they become debt free and generous cash millionaires. All while enjoying vigorous health, continued excellent income, advancing skill, a refined schedule, and an amazing family and personal life.

Here at WINNER**SEDGE** we have many sayings or "Toryisms" as people like to call them now. One of our favorites that you will hear at every seminar or training I do is this: *"We want it ALL!"* In other words, we want major success with everything in life. We want it ALL.

I have personally seen to it that we have not only the attitude, practice systems and resources, but also the money training and know-how to do this very well. All it takes is a coachable chiropractor. One with some drive and a strong desire to work.

Q: To Get a Little More Background, Did You Grow Up in A Chiropractic or Wealthy Family?

Nope. I grew up very middle class in Great Falls, Montana. My parents were divorced when I was around 11 years old. There was practically no affluence around me to model after. I have no memories of anything relating to money handling or prosperity.

I actually think this all worked to my advantage. I learned early that if I wanted something, I would have to go after it myself.

I remember as a kid I wanted a certain type of BMX bicycle. It never even occurred to me to ask anyone in my family to buy it for me because it would have been a joke to do so. My family was great, but I knew we didn't have money for extras like this. We had the essentials of course, but no disposable income you might say.

When I was old enough I became a paper boy. I was up delivering to 85 homes at 5:30 every Montana morning. What kid would do that today? I earned the money to buy the bike one part at a time. I will never forget the frame cost $115. Over several months I bought the forks, wheels, handlebars, seat, and pedals. Piece by piece I assembled and built it myself. I was so proud of that bike.

Little did I know, this would set the tone for the rest of my life. In fact, I think I was always a little jealous of the "rich kids" on the other side of town. It made me dream and want to work real hard so someday I could get whatever I wanted, whenever I wanted it.

I can't believe I found these pics. The REDLINE Pro Line bike. I'd give anything to know how many miles I put on that thing. On the right I'm wearing a Minnesota Vikings shirt. Decades later and 1000 miles away my office sits two blocks from the Vikings headquarters and practice field. Also on the right see the wood stove we used for heat. Notice the foil on the front, there to keep sparks from jumping out onto the carpet. Unreal.

Q: Briefly, So We Can Get to The Main Questions, How Did You Get to Where You Are Now?

Briefly? This could take an hour. Here it is in a nutshell: I graduated from high school and went to Montana State in Bozeman, Montana to become an architect. About half way through my freshman year I heard my dad say: *"Don't you know that architects starve?"* It made an impact so after my first year I joined the Air Force. (I grew up next to an Air Force base and loved the fighter jets my entire life.)

I worked it out so I could serve part-time in the Air Force, which allowed me to continue full-time at Montana State. I switched my major to Business and a couple semesters in I had good fortune come my way. I met a girl and her dad was a chiropractor. I really had no idea what a chiropractor even did back then.

Her parents came to town to visit and go to a football game. While visiting, her chiropractor dad used a Futon couch in her apartment and adjusted me. My lower back had been bothering me for some time so I thought it was awesome. He said: *"You oughtta think about becoming a chiropractor."* Now here I am.

His name was Dr. Bob Larson and he still practices in Billings, Montana. Funny thing, his daughters name was Tori. Mine is Tory. You can't make this stuff up! I was very proud to receive my Honorable Discharge from the Air Force, then graduate from MSU in Business. I had all the science requirements so off I went to Minneapolis and Northwestern College of Chiropractic.

I graduated from Northwestern and within 90 days was up and running in a brand-new office which I designed and built from literally a dirt floor. What made this possible

was a $36,000 home equity loan from my grandmother. I paid back every penny of that loan. Over the years I've realized just how unselfish she was to do this for me. She never could have paid that money back on her own. I have expanded several times since then and am now in the sixth office I have designed and built for myself. It's pretty cool.

I started consulting because of my practice success, ability to teach, and skill at "finding the way to win" for myself and others. It was also due to demand from other chiropractors and chiropractic students bugging me all the time to *"show them how to do it."* I created **WINNERSEDGE** Chiropractic Consulting with the simple mission to create and deliver the smartest, most effective, most relevant, and most complete chiropractic success training in the world via events, direct calls, audio, video, and written materials.

Interesting how the design and architecture training I had would end up being so valuable. Without any doubt I see my chiropractic office designs as the best in chiropractic today. You can tell a **WINNERSEDGE** designed office the second you step in one.

As far as the Air Force goes, this type of training affords me an incredible advantage. Military training teaches the planning, thoroughness, and precision rarely seen in the normal academic or working world. Not to mention it teaches a person what it really means to look sharp from head to toe.

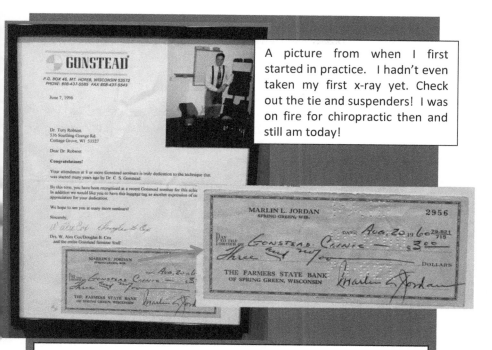

A picture from when I first started in practice. I hadn't even taken my first x-ray yet. Check out the tie and suspenders! I was on fire for chiropractic then and still am today!

I received this letter from The Gonstead Seminar for attending so many seminars. I have been to about 40 now. In my coaching, we have DCs doing everything from Nucca, Activator, Gonstead, Torque Release, you name it. On the bottom is a check to the Gonstead Clinic from 1960 that an older patient gave to me. She had Gonstead as her first chiropractor. It was just $3 to get adjusted back then! Notice the guy didn't even need to have his address on the checks.

Q: You Mention You Have Grown For 20 Years and Never "Flatlined" Or "Drifted." What Do You Mean?

A "flatlined" chiropractor is one whose practice has stopped growing. This can be caused by many things and if left uncorrected can lead to "drifting." A "drifting" doctor is one who is totally off the chiropractic or personal growth mission. Of course when asked they will *say* otherwise, but the truth is easy to see with a casual look at their practice and their life. Some chiropractors are so goofed-up and off track that even I can't fix them with all my success and re-charging tricks.

Famous quote by Henry David Thoreau: *"Most people lead lives of quiet desperation and go to the grave with most of their song still left in them."* It's pretty sad if this is describing a chiropractor.

I, on the other hand, preach a <u>relentless attack</u>. Constant and never ending improvement you might say. Perpetual on-mission goal striving. Every man or woman is either creating or disintegrating. Nothing <u>ever</u> stays the same in any area of life.

Q: Can You Explain Your LOVE, HEALTH, CAREER, And MONEY Concept? Where Did It Come From?

Here at WINNERSEDGE we simplify our goal setting down to four main areas of life: Love, Health, Career and Money. I'm not totally certain, but I think I first heard a man named Foster Hibbard talk about these on an old cassette tape. Sadly he left us a long time ago. Older doctors might remember him.

We will probably be talking a little more about money here today, but we absolutely can and should seek success and happiness in <u>all four areas</u>. Again remember our saying here: *We want it ALL!* For those who may be wondering, we include spiritual growth in the Love category. They are all critical areas to have goals in. I used to prioritize them in this order:

1. Love

2. Health

3. Career

4. Money

I was shockingly corrected at one seminar by a guest speaker. Legendary coach and Olympic gold medalist Dan Gable declared in front of the entire group that our order was all wrong and that he would change it! He went on to say that <u>all four of these elements in life are number one</u>!

1. Love   1. Health   1. Career   1. Money

Everyone was blown away, especially me. All attending were grateful for Gable's most intelligent observation and upgrade to our thought processes. He declared that your Love and relationships, Health and fitness, Career, and Money <u>are all equally important</u>. They ALL must be in place for a person to have a truly successful life. He also believed, and is living proof, that they can all work together. No one element has to be sacrificed for another.

Coach Gable basically said that there is no excuse for not working to succeed in all areas of life. *"You have to work at it"* he says. His life wisdom and massive experience with people was clearly evident. Gable, Jack Lalanne, Bob Proctor, and Demartini are the most impressive human beings I have ever personally met and talked with.

Me at the US Olympic Wrestling Team Trials with sports icon and legendary Coach Dan Gable, along with fellow friend, wrestling coach and chiropractic patient Bart Chelsevig. On the right, Gable at our Seminar. Gable did not win a gold medal, get voted one of the top 100 Olympians of all time, win 21 straight Big 10 Championships in a row, and become one of the top 3 coaches in American sports history by making or allowing excuses. **Question:** *Is what you do more important than any sport?*

Q: Speaking of Excuses, What Do You Think Of Them? Are They Common in Chiropractic?

Excuses, alibis, and blaming are all rampant in the world and common in chiropractic. Saying you *"don't have any money"* because you *"dedicated yourself to your family"* is an excuse and a lie. If you love your family you will make more money to take better care of them and their future. Is this not obvious?

If you do not religiously workout, and as a result you are physically "deconditioned," soft, and out of shape, then say it's because you *"don't have time"* this is an excuse and a lie. If you love yourself

13

and genuinely care about your patients and your family, then you will be in top physical condition. Is this not obvious? There really is no excuse for a chiropractor not leading by example.

> *"You can never expect a patient to get in better health than you are yourself."* –Bill Esteb

The most completely successful chiropractors are always physically conditioned. We must be physically and mentally superior for our patients, ourselves, and those we care about. We just have to.

Great saying: *"What you are speaks so loud I can't hear what you are saying."* This is so true. First impressions are so strong. People draw conclusions and form permanent opinions about you within seconds. If you can make good first impressions you are way ahead.

If you say you *"don't have time for seminars"* or *"don't have time to read"* it is just another weak excuse and a lie. Nothing that creates success takes any more time than anything else. The struggling chiropractor has the exact same amount of time as the super success.

Everyone has at least 112 waking hours every week. This is 6720 minutes. This is easily enough time to get everything done and done well. You have the same available minutes every week as me, every Nobel Prize winner, every company CEO, every NFL Head Coach, not to mention Edison, BJ Palmer, Picasso and everyone else. Time is abundant, but also very precious.

So unless a doctor is physically disabled and unable to practice, there is **no excuse.** We do not accept any excuses and neither should you. No lying to yourself. No alibis for why you are not doing better. Just admit the truth instead. It's the first step to growth.

All results are caused by an action, or inaction that created them. I chose everything in my life, and am now sitting in the results. All effects have a cause. I am the cause of all in my life. So are you. You are the cause. If you are happy that's great! We will grow from there.

If you are not as happy as you would like to be in any area of life there can be NO blaming, no being a crybaby, no looking for others to feel sorry for you. The late Nathaniel Branden would say: *"Nobody's coming."* Nobody's coming to rescue you or do anything for you.

You created your life and you are the only one who totally has the power to create your new and more successful future. Are you willing to pay the price? Do you know what the price is?

14

Interesting: A pic from my last office and the other from my new one. Countless times my car is the only one in the lot. When everyone else is sleeping, playing, and making their excuses, I am planning, creating, grinding and doing the hard mental work that very few have the discipline and will to tackle. This is what separates the super success from everyone else. There's a certain loneliness required to reach the high levels. If you are willing to pay this price you may get there. If you are not willing to pay the price... forget it.

Q: What Do You Consider as The First Step, Or Level of Money Success for The Chiropractor?

The doctor graduates from Chiropractic College, gets a state license, and now has the privilege to serve and earn in the health care world. The key word here is "privilege."

- The government calls it a "privilege." They can take it away very easily. It is important to appreciate how incredible the opportunity really is. Few in society ever have the power to own a business and especially the right to be able to bill insurance companies or Medicare. We must never take for granted how fortunate we are to be able to practice.

The first money level for all adults to reach is this: To earn enough from your own work and efforts to pay all your expenses with no help from anyone else. No loans deferred or requiring any borrowed money. This represents the most basic money level for an adult. This is the *"I can now fully support myself"* level. It is a great feeling. Many people and even some chiropractors struggle to ever get past this point.

Yes, an "entitlement" attitude can be present early on for a chiropractor. Society and the school system breed this ridiculous, underachieving, no work ethic, pain avoidance, unaccountable, sissified and pitiful mindset.

"Entitlement" means this:

- The DC *thinks* it should be easier.

- He or she *thinks* more new ones should just come in because they want them to, despite little or no effort.

- This chiropractor *thinks* people should simply hand them a credit card before actually delivering something of value first. *"You mean I actually have to work to get good at something before people will pay me for it? But I just want the money."*

- It hits them how hard it really is. They see it legitimately takes 10 times more effort and 10 times more work than they thought.

- They learn what expenses and responsibilities really are.

- The doctor realizes they now have to wake up every morning, and for the first time in their life figure out what to do. Suddenly there is no mommy, daddy, teacher or pre-set system in place to do their planning for them.

- When a doctor starts to make money another common mistake can occur. The doctor thinks the money they've collected is theirs to spend, and are shocked when they see their tax bill.

- Countless chiropractors end up behind on their taxes. This then takes an expert like myself and a good accountant to correct the mess. The proper systems must then be installed. More importantly, we must fix the chiropractor's backwards mind into understanding how chiropractic business really works.

- The newer chiropractor quickly realizes that school, parents, and their past experiences had no chance of preparing them for the much more vicious and unforgiving world they are now in.

- Sometimes a doctor can be suffering from "Something for nothing" syndrome and possibly "Quick fix" disease.

- The above mental errors are curable with strong and repetitive doses of WINNERSEDGE training.

This is the effort I am talking about. In an era where some DCs don't even own a quality plastic spine, I had the TV/DVD Player, neuropatholator, double bank viewbox, magnetic spine models stuck to the viewbox ready to go, strategically selected x-rays all lined up including larger pictures of gripping childbirth and spinal surgeries, the big white board, degeneration charts, a great model spine, and notice the poster below the whiteboard. It says right in front of everyone's face: *"We are a lifetime family practice. We care for you and your entire family from your first breath until your last. Or for as long as you want to be well."* This is how you go from a dirt floor, while only knowing 3 people in town, to 100 visits a day in 90 days. I said I was on a mission and my effort proved it. It has never been about money, it was about being a really good chiropractor. I was out to change lives and I still am!

It can be a sobering situation when a doctor is first struck by the reality of how life and business really work. There are many simple and even more hard lessons to learn in the process of growing.

Even more sobering is the person who is living on borrowed money and the borrowed money runs dry before the doctor has learned how, or put forth the effort required, to earn enough to cover all expenses. This is a terrifying feeling. One that is very motivating.

Some doctors simply fail to study and never really master the procedures. They don't read anything. They miss trainings and won't get the experiences that are absolutely required to cause growth. Doctors stuck in this mindset only do what is super convenient then wonder why they don't grow. Sad, since **the four enemies** are actually controlling the doctor vs. the doctor controlling them.

Q: What Are the Four Enemies of The Chiropractor?

The four enemies are: Laziness, weakness, cheapness, and foolishness. (Foolishness, if repeated, progresses to drifting and flat-out stupidness.) If any are present then massive emergency action must be taken to hammer the doctor into shape. We must get their mind, thoughts, and actions back into a state where success will be the result.

I have to work incredibly hard as a coach to get doctors through this, especially because I never had this issue. If anything, I knew I was going to have to give everything I had to make it. I expected it to be really hard. Failing would be an embarrassing disaster. For me there was one option and one option only, and that was to become a powerhouse chiropractor.

I expect nothing without having paid the price first. I know I will only get what I deserve in exact proportion to the mental and physical effort I have put in. *I am committed beyond convenience.*

Some Universal Laws I am referring to here are:
- What you sow you shall reap.
- Every cause brings its corresponding effect.
- Every action causes an equal and opposite reaction.
- Your income will always be equal to the value you give.
- You must give first before you will ever receive.

- You cannot get anything without paying the price.
- People's perception of who you are, is who you are.

The really successful chiropractor works to understand and comply with the many unwavering universal laws. Conversely, the not-so-successful man or woman spends their days and sometimes years trying to violate them, only to then blame everything except themselves for their lack of achievement.

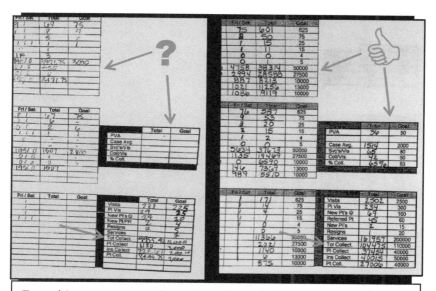

Two chiropractors send me their Goal and Stat sheet at the end of a month. Both DCs have been taught <u>exactly</u> how to do them. (Just know that clear goals are THE starting point for ALL success in practice.) Now compare the two. The DC on the left has no clear typed-in goals and has an incomplete, sloppy mess. If it were for a grade in any school it would get an "F." The DC on the right has clear typed-in goals, and a neat, complete sheet. This would get an "A." Who do you think is more successful? Look at the numbers. Looking at a chiropractor's goal and stat sheets is the same as looking directly into their mind. Complete, organized, and smart work comes from a clear, organized and smart mind. Sloppy, unclear, incomplete work comes from an, unclear, sloppy, and disorganized mind. *Which one are you?*

Q: Okay, A Doctor's Sheer Desire to Work Is the Core Issue. Now What Would You Say Brings the Next Level of Success?

You're right, we cannot talk about anything regarding practice success without <u>always</u> coming back to a doctor's sheer desire to work. Will the doctor put in the time? It is THE issue. Every chiropractor starts with some natural ability. A strong will to work is what brings the next levels of success. Always has been, always will be.

It starts with studying, memorizing the scripts, reading the recommended books, buying and listening to the CDs and attending the Seminars, Trainings, and Bootcamps. Working very hard on technique is also a basic requirement for success. Having a motivating coach and applying it all is the catalyst. This will grow a chiropractor to the level of manhood and womanhood required to win in practice.

The DC at the next level is now earning enough to cover all practice and personal expenses <u>plus</u> has installed the WINNER**SEDGE** Money Flow plan including the ***Rapid Fire*** Debt Elimination System.

The WINNER**SEDGE** money flow system <u>must be in place</u>. Sometimes we call it **the underlying money flow architecture of the chiropractor.** This is the invisible, yet very real underlying system of money channeling required for greater financial success.

It all starts with clear goals, which is why we do an ORANGECARD at every seminar. Every chiropractor must always have a definite chief aim and clear goals in all four areas of life.

Q: Whoa You Lost Me, What Is an Orange Card?

The ORANGECARD is one of my earliest inventions. It would take a while to explain its history in detail.

The starting point for all success is having clear, accurate, written down goals in the key categories of life. As Brian Tracy says: ***"Goals are everything, all else is just commentary."***

Years ago I would write my goals down on a scrap piece of orange card stock paper. I would carry this card in my wallet. Once I reached these goals I would write a new set of goals on a new piece of orange card stock paper. I would carry the new card in my wallet.

I taught this to a few success minded friends and they started to reach all of their goals too. Some started to call me the "orange card guy." I knew I had something very unique, very powerful, and probably never before done at any chiropractic seminar. I actually named my first seminars the "ORANGECARD Seminar." They revolved around teaching people exactly how to create and write out their goals.

I have modified what the card looks like since then. Now at every WINNERSEDGE seminar, during the second hour I teach the ORANGECARD training. Everyone makes a warm, shiny, new ORANGECARD. Those who have one will know what I mean by warm. There is a very specific way to create the front of the card, and an even more specific way to create the back of the card.

It takes about an hour to properly create an ORANGECARD. Every WINNERSEDGE member always has clear goals on their card. They carry it in their wallet like I teach. It is one of many unique tools I use to keep every doctor and CAs mind on the precise goals they want to see become real in their practice and in their life.

The best advice I could give anyone whether chiropractor or other success seeker is to <u>always have well engineered and clearly written down goals</u>. Then plant them in your wallet.

Here's something most people would never see. I dug out a few vintage ORANGECARDs. The front two are the front and back of the latest version. On the right is my current card in the Tumi wallet I recommend for all men. Women change wallets often so they are on their own. Wallets and purses are a very important part of your image, much more important than most realize.

Q: Wow That's Really Cool, How Do I Get One of Those Cards?

The only way to get an ORANGECARD is at one of our Seminars. If you are endorsed by a current member, or by me personally, we will let you attend one. No outsiders are ever allowed at our other events.

Q: Okay Tory, Will You Tell Us What the WINNERSEDGE Money Flow System Is?

Sure, I will teach you this for a million bucks! Actually, it is worth more than this over the course of a typical 40-year chiropractic career. The WINNERSEDGE Money Flow System is our foundational tool for all chiropractors who want to be happy, successful, and wealthy. It is something I never teach outside my group, but I agreed to answer these questions so I will lay it out as clearly as I can. Pay attention.

What you are going to learn here may seem simple after you read it. It may even seem easy. Reading stuff is easy. Going and flat-out doing it is what separates the winners from the posers. Be a winner!

It will have components and ideas that will make sense to you. You may even have bits and pieces of it already in place.

Some might even dismiss it and think what they are doing is "just as good." It probably isn't. As you learn this system, really see its many benefits. Ponder what it could bring you years from now if you actually install it into your life. Compare it to what you might have years from now if you keep the system you are currently using.

Here are several reasons why this system is so valuable:

1. It makes sure your taxes are current to the week. This does a few key things:

    a. It eliminates the ever present, hidden self-sabotage, and negative charge that people have about paying taxes.

    b. It is very hard to get behind on your taxes if you pay them weekly like I teach. Paying taxes monthly or quarterly is only for doctors who don't know any better, or who are not making much money. Waiting for a tax bill at the end of the year practically guarantees eternal poverty.

2. The system makes sure you are <u>giving money away consistently</u>. Giving money away = planting money seeds. They will return a harvest. If you want a bigger harvest then plant more seeds. <u>Whatever you want more of in life, you must give away first.</u> No giving = no receiving.

3. It guarantees <u>your debt reduction is dramatically accelerated</u>. Your debt is being attacked weekly or even daily. It will vanish much faster than if handled conventionally.

4. It guarantees <u>you are saving money weekly</u>. You've established the habit of saving. Ingrain this saying: ***"The first part of all you earn is yours to keep!"***

5. Getting your money handling in order <u>will actually cause your practice to grow</u>. If a doctor does not have perfect money flow and money handling, then it will "constipate" their entire practice. Money flow must be fixed first. It will unlock and allow more people and money to flow to you and your office.

   o Most doctors are attempting to do a lot of marketing to try and grow. They are totally blind to the fact that <u>they will never grow until their money flow is corrected</u> and perfectly organized first.

   o If you cannot lift a 30lb weight easily, you will never be trusted to lift the 40lb. If you cannot handle, be current and ahead with $30k per month, you will never reach and be trusted with $40k+ per month.

   o A chiropractor will grow to their level of financial organization and money flow systems.

   o I am able to double, triple, or quadruple many client practices without ever talking about new patients or marketing. Remember, <u>money flow is THE critical underlying architecture of ALL businesses including your practice.</u>

6. Having our money system in place allows you to sleep well at night knowing you actually have a plan that will bring your future prosperity. Almost no doctors have such a plan.

Here are the basic elements of the system. It would take a couple hours for me to draw it out for you and cover all the details, but this will give you the idea.

The WINNERSEDGE Money Flow System:

1. The doctor is paid weekly and it is automated electronically. This means the money automatically comes out of the clinic account and the next day it goes in the doctors personal account.

2. Triggered by this weekly paycheck, the estimated state and federal tax deposits for the doctor are also automated and paid weekly. This means the federal and any state tax is electronically and automatically paid every single week.

3. Staff payroll is automated every two weeks.

4. Payroll taxes are automated every two weeks triggered by the staff payroll. Again this is automatically and electronically done. All the clinic owner sees are the email confirmations.

5. Giving is automated every month to whatever cause or causes the doctor desires. Again remember: *No giving = no receiving.*

6. Savings is automated every week via online Bill Pay.

7. The debt list is created and the WINNERSEDGE *Rapid Fire* debt elimination system is engaged.

8. After all these are completed, then and only then can a doctor spend a penny on anything else.

9. Complete separation of business and personal expenses is absolutely essential. Regularly spending clinic money on personal anything is the sure-fire way to be broke forever.

   - In my wallet I carry only a personal checking account debit card. Only if I am specifically buying something for my business, or traveling for business related action, will I ever carry a business credit or debit card.

The architecture and flow must be in place, even with small amounts. If you can only save $10 a week and donate $10 per month then fine! **The key is the SYSTEM.** No system = no chance of success.

Your office must have a system for new patients, a system for reports, a system for the ideal office visit, a system for payroll, a system for taxes.

I am writing this and you are listening because I have incredibly smart and proven systems that always work.

The doctor has enough to worry about every day, so **as much as possible must be automated via a system**. My entire payroll and accounting system amounts to about 8 emails every month.

Let me explain:

- Every Monday morning my accountant sends me an email telling me: *"Your paycheck will come out of your business account today and go into your personal account tomorrow. Your state and federal tax deposits will be automatically paid on Thursday."*

- Every two weeks I send my accountant an email with my staff hours. They send back an email with the paystubs attached reporting: *"The money will come out of the business account today, and go into the employee accounts on Wednesday. The payroll taxes will be automatically sent on Thursday."*

- At months-end I will get an email with the clinic accounting statements, and in my case another attachment with my consulting accounting statements. I save them all in a folder.

- My total time spent every month on payroll and accounting is maybe 30 minutes because I have engineered a SYSTEM.

- As many bills as possible are automated via online Bill Pay.

- What you see here will work 100% of the time for every person who engages it properly. You can do it.

- When your taxes are current, your debt is being crushed, and you are saving all simultaneously, believe me, it is only a matter of time before you see significant net worth changes.

- Incredibly profound statement: ***"Spend less than you make."***

Now just let this sink in for a minute. What you see here is how it is done if you want to reach the higher levels. Automation is the key. We <u>must</u> remove the chiropractors behavioral weaknesses from the equation. It is a system that must be forced into place. You have got to get your hands OFF the money if you ever want to end up with any.

At this point I must say: I'm not the least bit interested in what anyone else does or teaches regarding money handling for chiropractors. I especially don't care what any financial advisor, insurance salesman, accountant, or other scorpion parasite in my profession thinks.

This is how I do it. It works better than anything I have ever seen any other chiropractor do. I challenge anyone to find a smarter, simpler, more complete, and more efficient money system anywhere. I recommend elevating to it.

As you read this it will make sense and might even look easy. You might find it is harder to put in place than you think. Of course all that is good and truly powerful can be more difficult to accomplish than expected. Like many things, if it were easy everyone would do it.

Now, you must be the one to engineer this. You are the one who gets the accountant to do what you need done. You must get them to do things your way and not their dopey way. Even though it seems pretty straightforward, most accountants cannot do what I teach here.

We have this system because of its ability to help us reach our financial goals much faster. Accountants and many others do not understand or care about our goals. They only know the easiest way to do what their system allows with your money.

See, those who are not *empowered* when it comes to handling money will ALWAYS be *overpowered* by others when it comes to handling money. *The rich get richer* is the saying we all know. It is true.

What you see here is 20 years worth of work and refining. It requires an accountant who understands what we are trying to accomplish financially and the challenges we face in trying to eliminate debt and accumulate money.

If you do not have the right accountant you will never get ahead. You + Your consultant + Your accountant comprise your success team.

It is worth stating here that very few chiropractors have any real money. Most chiropractors think, talk, and behave like poor people. Very few think, talk, and act like rich people. **Only listen to those who truly are experts when it comes to anything money related**. Piles of untested ideas and dead-end opinions are everywhere out there.

I have described the key elements so far. Things can get more complex, but usually the more complex you get the more ripped off you get. Never underestimate the power of simplicity. <u>Love simplicity.</u>

Q: Amazing. I Am Going to Have To Study This. Now What Is the *Rapid Fire* Debt System?

I invented the WINNER**SEDGE** *Rapid Fire* Debt Elimination System by accident. I have never seen or heard of anything like it anywhere. This is another secret weapon normally never taught to anyone outside my group. Since you want to be a winner financially and in life, let me cover it here for you.

I will be brief since this topic could easily take 10 pages and a two-hour CD set to explain in more detail.

I had been paying over $1000 per month on my student loans for about 10 years. I initially owed $128,000. (Not much by today's insane student loan standards.) Observe I had paid in over $100,000. It was all automated. I never received any statements. I thought all was cool.

One day I was curious what I still owed so I logged in for the first time. Expecting to be happy, since I knew I had paid in a ton, I discovered that I still owed $123,000! **What?**

I had paid in $100,000 towards a $128,000 debt and still owed $123,000? This means only $5000 went towards the principal and $95,000 was all interest! Are you kidding me? Do you get the idea how interest really works now?

When you see a loan for 5% interest, it is more like 90% when you really understand that the percentage rate quoted is simply a numerical factor involved in calculating what they are really going to make you pay. The way the loans are structured and front loaded is very complex and downright evil to say the least.

I was mad. Mad at myself because I knew I had collected enough over the past 10 years in practice to have them paid already. What I did was this: I kept the regular monthly payment rolling as per usual. I grabbed a business card and on the back I wrote these words: **PAY SOME NOW.** I then stuck this card in my computer keyboard where the function keys are so it would be in my face every day.

What I did next was make a payment <u>every single day</u> and sometimes even two or three payments a day. $500, then $100 more at lunch, then maybe $50 at night. If it was a good collections day I would send $2000 or even $5000. Then if the time was lean maybe only $5. Day after day <u>religiously and with reckless abandon</u> I did this. I smashed the pedal to the floor and was on a mission. I started this in

January and guess what? I had the loans gone in August. I dusted $123,000 of life sucking debt in under 9 months. My practice grew the entire time. The key to know is that <u>I never missed the money.</u>

The mathematical technology and the universal laws that are at work in this process are remarkable and astonishing.

I have so much to say about how cool this is I could easily write another small book on this topic. I doubt I have to explain to anyone why paying off debt is awesome, so I will just tell you how to do it.

1. Get the **WINNERSEDGE** Money Flow System in place FULLY or as much as possible for now.

2. Taxes are automated weekly for the doctor and bi-weekly for all staff. Giving, saving, and debt are automated as taught.

3. Now line up all debts from smallest to largest. A debt is something that you can actually pay off early. Some leases do not qualify since many leases cannot be paid off early.

4. Automate the regular monthly payment on ALL debts.

5. Then pick the smallest debt. Yes, the smallest debt. You <u>do not care about interest rates</u>. What you are after is freeing up the payment as fast as you can, so you always go after the smallest debt first. Paying off the smallest debts first builds momentum.

6. Once all the small debts are paid in full, we then attack the larger practice and personal debts. **<u>Do this by making the regular payment plus another weekly payment that is automated.</u>** Push the system, if the payments are easy you are <u>not</u> doing it

right. In addition to this you can make a payment every day like I did if you want to make them vanish even faster.

7. The true **Rapid Fire** is you sending a payment <u>every single day</u>!

8. A doctor can reach the level where all equipment loans are paid, all leases are done, all other debt like money owed to family, credit cards, past taxes, and the x-ray machine are all handled forever. This is an incredible feeling!

Some money "gurus" out there talk about the need for an "emergency fund." Emergency funds only cause emergencies to happen. I see no reason for any chiropractor to have such a thing.

With heavy interest accruing against you every day, there is no time to waste. Get all extra money going towards debt. We have receivables and credit cards in the rare case where hell breaks loose.

It is a relief to have a system that practically guarantees your taxes are always current, while you are simultaneously crushing debt, saving money, and giving a little away.

The best part is the automated giving to a charity or cause. This is a true secret to creating wealth. Give = receive. Another Toryism is: *"Hurry up and make some money already so you can give more away and make a difference in the world."*

Additional money details and reminders:

- Car payments should for sure be automated weekly also.
  - **Example**: If the car payment is $450. Pay $150 a week. Then ignore it as auto loans are short term loans anyway. Plus, <u>you normally save no interest by paying an auto loan early</u>. Then once paid in full keep the car for at least a few more years as you crush debt.

- State and federal is tax automated weekly. Possibly monthly at lower levels. <u>Never</u> quarterly or at years end. All taxes including payroll taxes are always current. The rich DC never waits to pay tax. The poor DC is behind and has no real system.

Still at this level the doctor can commonly be caught thinking "me me me" and that outer circumstances create their life. Alibis, excuses and blaming can still be present. Ex-wives, ex-husbands, past business associates, or whoever is usually blamed for the DCs problems.

Of course, the DC, just like everyone else, is actually the real cause of everything occurring in their money life. As soon as they just admit it and see this fact then growth immediately occurs. **Blaming = powerless. Taking responsibility = POWER!**

- Know how much of your student loan payment is interest and how much is principal. *Pay enough to bite the principal.* The low-level doctor does not even know if they are covering the interest on their student loans. Even lower level is the DC who has loans deferred. Some denial on the part of the chiropractor may have yet to be conquered. You owe it, get after paying it.

- As any debt pays-off, the payment money you freed up is called **"found money"** and must immediately be applied to the next debt. *Do this immediately or your income will drop by the same amount!* You must keep the pressure on the money system.

- The better a chiropractor is at handling money + the more clear their goals are + the more they are on a mission = the more money will come to them. A LAW that never varies. *"Money comes to those who hath."*

Here a shakedown occurs. The real doers emerge, rise to the top and distance themselves from their classmates. These doctors know that the more uncomfortable they are the more they will grow. The more difficult or inconvenient something is, the more they will grow.

The advancing doctor goes to away seminars when they "don't feel like it" and they do bootcamps that they know are hard and they send their team to training events (even though they'd rather buy something or save the money for themselves). They watch videos, take notes, and really start to effectively apply knowledge.

- Every person must learn: If you want anything = you MUST pay. And pay more than you think. Pay more than the lesser DC understands or ever is willing to. This is what truly separates the big from the perpetually small. Pay more = get more. The lesser DC thinks that the little they pay is a lot, only because they don't know what a lot really is. We are here to prove it is worth it.

The more successful chiropractor understands that success is a matter of trading small amounts of money first, in order to get a bigger return later. The less successful DC is always worried about cost.

Q: Some DCs Get Involved with Other Things to Try and Make Money. What Do You Think of This?

Do you mean things like real estate, doing IMEs, decompression, lasers, orthotics, weight loss, multilevel? These are all out there. I personally feel they are all distractions. These are avenues where doctors who are bad at math can lose a ton of money and momentum.

Let me say a few words about multilevel. If it has not already reared its cancerous head, DCs will have to confront the inevitable introduction to multilevel marketing. The serious chiropractor will see through the formula they all use where one token person (who is incredibly talented, lucky, or had an incredibly unique situation that will never happen with you) has made it big and is now getting you to think you can do the same.

Their great "opportunity" usually pays a Stanford or Harvard MD or PhD, and possibly a celebrity or athlete if they can afford it, to get them to endorse their products or whatever else they are selling. Their favorite line is: *"The products sell themselves"* or some other lie that they have gotten themselves to believe and then spew all over you.

Normally I would never care. There are some who are extremely gifted in sales and persuasion who might be able to do alright in multilevel. However, I start to care in a hurry when they bash or minimize chiropractic. Some try to derail a doctor into thinking that they need to do something in addition to practicing or worse yet, instead of practicing.

I'm ready to call out my fire breathing Dobermans at even the thought of this horrible use of the power of suggestion.

- The idea of easy residual income is preached, yet the person preaching it usually has no real money. The smart doctor easily sees there is no real chance at this.

- It commonly violates one or two State Board rules.

- Why a doctor with a $200,000+ education would waste one second on something that people with no education can do is a mystery to me.

- Maybe the doctor just sucked at chiropractic, sold out, was broken, and errantly thought there was an easier way to the money tree. It proves the chiropractor was never fully dedicated.

The word here is **HONOR**. In my opinion it is not honorable for a chiropractor to have any agenda in their chiropractic office other than delivering chiropractic awesomeness to a lot of people.

Q: Can You Explain What You Mean By "Honor?"

We must understand the <u>real cost</u> of everything. Any opportunity that may be presented must have ALL its real costs analyzed carefully. A doctor must look at **the real cost** or have all the real costs clearly shown to them by someone like me. They will quickly see that <u>there is nothing they could ever do with their time that is more powerful, more profitable, and more valuable in the future than building a large dynamic practice.</u>

<u>Nothing</u> is any easier. **There is no way to escape the work.** There is no way to get a greater return somewhere else with less work. If you want to earn $500,000 in real estate it will take the <u>exact same amount of work</u>, and effort, and pain, and losses, and frustrations, and time, and risk as it would to make $500,000 in chiropractic or anything else. Really understand this truth of life and compensation. I recommend a doctor stay with what they know! That is the phenomenon known as chiropractic. Delivering incredible chiropractic care to the masses. There is no easier way!

Stay the course, be steady, have the clear goals we teach here and go go go. Toryism: *When in doubt, smash on the gas!*

I am proud of a few things. One is that I never deviated from the chiropractic mission. I am 100% dedicated for life to chiropractic and helping as many doctors as possible become super successful while living the incredible chiropractic lifestyle.

Honor is such an important word. How many people of honor are out there today? I'd rather die with honor than with a billion dollars.

"You can say a lot of things about a man or a woman. They were rich or they were broke. They were smart or they weren't so smart. They were good looking or they weren't so good looking. But there is no better thing you can say about a man or a woman than they were a person of their word. When they said they were going to do something they did it. There are very few people in the world today you can say that about. But damn it you're gonna be able to say that about me."

-Evel Knievel

Honor: ˈänər/

noun

1. a keen sense of ethical conduct
2. one whose worth brings respect
3. good quality or character as judged by others
4. high moral standards of behavior
5. one's word given as a guarantee of performance

Me and my boy Indy, a purebred European Doberman. His grandpa is considered the top male Doberman in the world. He will lick your face and love you every time you walk in the door. He'll be excited when you are excited and sad when you are sad. And... if you are scared he will protect you with a vicious wall of muscle and teeth, and he will do it with everything he has until his last breath. He doesn't have to be taught how to be fearless, or dedicated, or determined, or loyal, or to stand for something, or to stay in shape. He knows what **honor** is. This is how I feel about chiropractic and about my clients. We call it the WINNERS**EDGE** Doberman Philosophy. In fact, I have even been called the Chiropractic Doberman because of my promotion of this philosophy in myself and in my consulting with other doctors.

A few questions for chiropractors:

1. *Are you an honorable chiropractor?*

2. *Does being a man or woman of honor matter to you?*

3. *Are you worthy of respect or are you criticized? What really is your reputation among your family, friends, patients, and fellow chiropractors? Oh yes – it matters.*

4. *If you had a kid grow up to be a chiropractor would you want them to be just like you?*

5. *Is it just about the money or do you actually want to be great at something?*

Q: When Do You Think a Chiropractor Should Consider Buying a Home?

Possibly never. It might shock a few people but my official position is: Don't even think of buying a home until your student loans are paid in full. *Student loans are a mortgage, why add another?* Buying a home before all small and larger debt is completely paid, or close to it, is just a set up for massive losses.

If you buy too much home too early, you'll dig yourself a hole so deep it will take years to climb out of it.

Understand these facts:

1. A home is not an asset. It is an asset to the bank.

2. An asset puts money in your wallet every month. A home takes money out of your wallet every month. Lots of it.

3. A home brings what are called **phantom payments.** Never forget this term! More positively stated: Always remember the reality of **phantom payments.**

4. **Phantom payments** are the endless expenses that never go away when owning a home.

5. Thus a home will cost up to double the monthly mortgage payment. **Read carefully,** this means your $1800 per month home is really going to take $3000 to $3600 out of your life

every month. <u>Nobody will ever tell you this</u> because it may deter you from being another victim of the home buying racket. The biggest reason home buying exists is to create more debt for banks. If you don't pay guess what happens? The bank takes your house. A great deal for them.

6. Whatever house you can afford early on is almost never the one you want to end up in. Why even buy it then?

Here's a story:

A couple buys their first home, a lovely new 4 bedroom 3 bath two story in a nice new development. It is move-in ready but comes with no deck on the back. The board is there on the back of the house to attach the deck to, but no deck. *"We'll get to that deck later"* they say as they smile and excitedly move in.

Of course, the nice mortgage lady at the bank has loaned them all they wanted to "buy" the house. The payment is $2200 per month. *"No problem"* they comment as they look at their combined income. *"This is awesome"* they say as they settle in!

Now... **like a vapor, the phantom payments slowly and silently slither in one at a time**... The homeowner's insurance, the window treatments, the yard, the garage supplies, the mower, the neighborhood association dues, another trip to Home Depot, the first repairman for the new fridge that somehow isn't cold, the basketball hoop, the nicer furniture, bigger TV, another trip to Menards, on and on.

Six months into this new life their income is totally consumed every month. The home costs $2200 per month <u>but their new life in this home costs over $3200 every month</u>. They are now tapped out.

Forget accelerating any debt. Instead, they break out the credit cards for many different expenses. Now this brings larger credit card payments every month on top of everything else.

The next "great decision" sounds like this: *"Honey, let's get a home equity loan and use the equity we have to pay off our credit cards and other small debts."* The couple is all excited. They are going to pay off those pesky smaller debts and move them into a second mortgage. Aren't they "smart?" Now they have added this additional long-term debt into their life. The payment on this home equity line is just interest only. They figure they will pay more towards it later.

Guess what happens next in nearly every case? They have another "emergency" and just *"have to use"* their credit cards. Now they again have the credit card payments PLUS the home equity loan payment, PLUS the mortgage, all with interest of course.

And the house sits with no deck on the back because they were going to: *"Get to that deck later."*

If you look closely you will start to see the stress in both their eyes. It starts to hit them they are not getting ahead. They may look okay from the street, but inside they know they have no money accumulation and no chance of paying down any debt with any speed any time soon. They "hope" it will just get better down the road.

They have been caught in the *monthly payment trap.* They thought if they could just afford the monthly payments, that they could afford whatever it was they were buying. **This may be the biggest money mistake in the world today.** Everything has extra costs.

"Watch your step honey."

I drove through five different neighborhoods on the way to my office. They've all been there for years. **What does this tell you? Will you learn from it?** Are you going to be smart and do things right, or be a fool and have to *"Get to that deck later?"*

Their lifestyle, dictated by the house, was beyond what they could <u>truly afford</u>. They did not know about or account for the ***phantom payments***. When you buy a house you don't just pay for a house. You pay for a lifestyle. ALWAYS remember this.

Q: Is It a Conspiracy?

Does a one-legged duck swim in a circle? Of course, it's a conspiracy! The big four are out to get you! The manufacturers make stuff, then the merchants sell stuff, then the advertising industry goes to work on your mind to get you to think you need the stuff, and finally the credit industry smiles as they give you the kiss of death by offering you a way to "pay for the stuff" via their life destroying and poverty causing low monthly payments.

They are all working together to steal every penny you ever make in your entire lifetime. That's all. Their highly organized and continuous efforts are working every minute of every day to lure my money from me, and your money away from you.

Q: What Else as Far as Houses Go?

We must be very smart and have good timing. You are now aware of phantom payments. Pay attention, be aware, be smart and please don't be foolish. <u>Obey the laws of human behavior and economics.</u> Please KNOW that EVERYTHING you do can and certainly will cost twice what the <u>front number</u> is.

If you can handle double whatever the front number is on any expense with a monthly payment you will probably be okay.

Consider:

- Rent a small cheap place close to work.

- Pay down debt like crazy.

- Of course auto saving the entire time.

- Enjoy the "someone else has to worry about it" joys of renting.

- Only if actually needed, maybe move into a nicer rental. Apartment, condo, home with big yard, whatever. You can rent anything out there. Keep it cheap.

- Understand that buying a home is the same as renting but costs a ton more. If you have a mortgage, believe me, you are still renting.

- The word mortgage is derived from the words mortuary and mortician. It means "death clutch."

- Debt comes from the word death. Pay off all smaller debts and then really attack the student loan monster.

- As the student loans are almost gone and are under $20,000 then start looking at homes. Get the mind preparing and visualizing. Again, only if you need it, want one, and plan to stay there for a long time.

- Once all debt is gone, buy the right home and stay there. Otherwise, I recommend you just rent.

- Never buy into the common notion that you can deduct the home mortgage interest off on your taxes. This deduction usually amounts to nothing.

- Also, never buy the idea that homes appreciate. Those days are over and would never be something you would want to count on anyway.

- The typical American family moves every 7 years. This means that every 7 years they start out again at the beginning of the heavy interest front loaded amortization schedule. After 21 years they have yet to even touch the principal on their mortgage. They should have just rented.

- Never let anyone tell you that you are throwing money away by renting. The amount you save from all the extra home expenses and phantom payments is nearly always more than whatever equity you *thought* you would build over the same time period.

- We buy a home because we want and need one. Until then, you want and need to pay off other debt first.

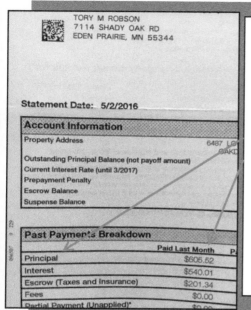

TORY M ROBSON
7114 SHADY OAK RD
EDEN PRAIRIE, MN 55344

Statement Date: 5/2/2016

Account Information

Property Address	6487 L...
Outstanding Principal Balance (not payoff amount)	
Current Interest Rate (until 3/2017)	
Prepayment Penalty	
Escrow Balance	
Suspense Balance	

Past Payments Breakdown

	Paid Last Month	P
Principal	$606.52	
Interest	$540.01	
Escrow (Taxes and Insurance)	$201.34	
Fees	$0.00	
Partial Payment (Unapplied)*	$0.00	

I paid all clinic debt, all credit cards, all student loans, all car loans before buying my first property, which I still own as a rental. Here is a mortgage statement. After 10 years of owning this property the interest is still $540 per month.

The rate on this mortgage is a decent 3.95% yet each month <u>after 10 years</u> I am still paying what looks like 47% in interest? Is there something going on here? YES, the interest rate is the <u>front number</u> but behind the scenes the math is stacked heavily against us.

There is nothing noble about buying a home. If you are already loaded with debt, you might reconsider. In my consulting, I witness the home buying urge is more prevalent in women. Many times the guy involved doesn't care as much but *"she wants to buy a house."* Be careful and make decisions based on math, not emotion.

The "American dream" is actually the Bankers dream so consider just renting. Be happy until it is time to do it right and buy or build THE home you plan to stay in for decades.

Buying a home is such an expensive and sticky situation that it must be done right. Get the house you really want when the time is right. Once you are in the right home your next task will be to set up your home command center. Make sure it is super organized like your clinic.

A home is a small corporation and should run like one. Bill paying, expenses, banking, insurances, and all other home expenses must be in order. You want a clinic in perfect order and the home in perfect order. Run a "tight ship" as some would say.

Q: Do You Have Any More Key Money Points You Want to Talk About?

Here's a few that come to mind:

- When you <u>force</u> debt elimination more money comes to you.

- When you lock into a money goal it happens a lot faster.

- Paying from $50,000 to zero on a debt goes a lot faster than from paying from $100,000 down to $50,000. Do you know why?

- The more you pay down a debt, the faster it goes down as each payment eats a little more principal. This then lowers the amount of interest that accrues against you.

- The banks want you to pay everything monthly. What does that tell you? It is best for <u>them</u>. They want to get all the interest for the month. This is why we have the WINNER**SEDGE** principle of: *Small amounts weekly.*

- Once you learn to pay small amounts weekly towards debt or savings you will be amazed at what happens. *The frequency you send payments is the key.* Just start doing it!

- It works on a mysterious phenomenon where <u>everyone has a little fluff money in their life every day</u>. You are simply sucking this money out and immediately using it towards a debt before this money vanishes on something useless.

- The momentum this creates is significant. When a debt pays off you then include that found money into your payment on the next debt. <u>You can crush a lot of debt a lot faster than you think!</u>

- The speed that you can send money with online banking is the secret weapon. Use it to your advantage.

- It works the same for saving and accumulating as it does for debt. **Example**: When it is time to buy a home you can save more money faster by saving weekly per the ***Rapid Fire*** concept.

- Again, it is a system. **Systems are the real key.** There is nothing difficult about having more things in your life automated, eliminated, delegated, or down to a system.

- When you handle money better, more money will flow to you because you have proven you can handle it effectively. *You will hear this over and over from me.*

- Again, if you cannot lift a 40lb dumbbell easily, nobody will ever hand you the 50lb and say *"try this."* Money is exactly the same. If you cannot easily and properly handle all the money in your life right now, you will <u>never</u> get any more to handle.

- More money only brings you more of what you already have. If you have a lot of debt and stress, more money will only increase your debt and stress. If you are happy and organized with your money, more money will only magnify this.

- It is idiocy when a poor money handler thinks that more money will fix their problems. <u>The only thing that will ever fix a money mess are completely upgraded money skills and money handling disciplines.</u>

Q: How Do You Know If You Are Not Good at Handling Money? It Seems Everyone Thinks They Are Decent Money Handlers.

Great point. Everyone thinks they know how to "handle money." What they really mean is that they know how to "spend money." There is a BIG difference. Very few have true mastery with debt elimination and money accumulation, probably including the reader of this page.

A good money handler has all money systems in impressive order like I teach. They always seem to have money and are relaxed about money and money issues. They are the doctors you meet who just seem to be a step ahead of everyone else.

As a chiropractor, you are a money mess if:

- Your taxes are not <u>perfectly</u> current.

- Your payroll taxes are not <u>perfectly</u> current.

- You don't know what your net income really is. Instead you have an "imaginary" budget.

- You ever have to file an extension on your taxes.

- You have any balances on department store credit cards.

- You are not auto-saving every week <u>religiously</u>.

- You are not giving and donating money to one or more worthwhile causes <u>every month automatically</u>.

- You owe money or ever borrow from family members.

- You are behind on payments for anything.

- You try to buy things to look cool, using credit.

- You want people to pay you on time and get mad if they don't, yet you fail to pay others on time.

- You over tip to look like a bigshot.

- You are cheap when it comes to tips in restaurants, or with donations or similar opportunities. (Quick lesson: *Always over tip breakfast wait staff.*)

- You ever fight with anyone over money.

- You say you will *"worry about saving for retirement later."*

- You feel you have something to hide when it comes to your financial life.

- You say things like: *"I don't know where the money goes."*

- You borrow money via credit for vacations.

- You borrow money via credit at Christmas time.

- You let a spouse get away with terrible money habits that affect the entire household. Worse yet, you think their bad money habits are *"cute."*

- You think that a coffee every day is fine because: *"It only costs $3 bucks."*

- You feel that more money is what will fix your problems.

- You are happy when money things are good, then you are down if money things are not good. The yo-yo syndrome.

- You think that learning about money is boring or that you *"don't need it."*

- You could not make it more than a month or two if your income stopped.

- You don't save all your receipts or have organized and labeled files for everything. You say it is because you *"haven't gotten to it yet."*

- You have a habit of buying personal things with clinic money.

- You have a credit score under 700.

- You've made excuses for any of the above.

Keep in mind everyone has different money concepts and different goals. Everyone has differing abilities to earn. A person with good money skills may have very little money because of their weak money concepts and self-worth issues.

Some have a huge self-image and earn a LOT of money, yet are a money mess. Choose to earn a lot of money <u>and</u> handle it well!

I will mention here: It is very important to be sharp if others <u>owe you money</u>. Demand integrity from others. A great quote by Jim Rohn: *"Keep strict accounts."*

Q: So What Are Smart Money Priorities?

Once a chiropractor is earning more and **wanting to move up the money handling ladder,** an entirely new error in judgement can and often does emerge. A chiropractor can start to think they are "special" and that they "have money." This chiropractor begins to buy things they really cannot afford. It happens because ego overrides prudence.

A false sense of success tragically can express itself. The doctor starts trying to *"look rich"* or *"be cool"* yet is not saving any real money. The doctor is not paying enough on debt and many times even owes back taxes. Their money system is actually completely upside down. <u>The upside down money flow mess represents almost all of America and everyone you know</u>, including many chiropractors.

Let me go over the order of priorities in money handling of the POOR chiropractor compared to the RICH chiropractor.

It is good to have many examples of what not to think, not to do, and not be like. Once you know <u>what NOT to do</u> it is easier to then learn <u>what TO do.</u>

Contrasting good and bad is important in gaining a complete understanding. You must be able to see mistakes in others and more importantly, you must be able to see mistakes that you are making and correct them. I call it being able to "police yourself."

Order of priorities for the POOR chiropractor:

1. Concerned about bringing increase to themselves.
2. Buying stuff "they want."
3. Essential expenses to stay open and alive.
4. The minimum monthly payments they have to pay.
5. Taxes they have to pay.
6. Payroll taxes maybe.
7. Extra on debt if any money is left, but there never is.
8. Saving if any money is left, but there never is.
9. Giving if they have any left, but they never do.

These people always think they *"need more money"* and that more money will fix their problems. They call and say they *"need more new ones"* and complain about taxes, insurance companies and everything else. Yet on the outside you see them making Facebook posts about their "awesome life" and their cool stuff.

I knew this life for a while until I had my ass handed to me via several encounters with people more successful than I was. I noticed they spoke differently. They carried themselves differently. They handled money a lot differently than I did. Their life showed it. It was a lot more solid and on a better track than mine at the time.

I decided to go on a financial education rampage and decreed to become a money handling master. I started by listening to audios in the car. I read *The Richest Man In Babylon* by George Clason. I must say that the first time I read it I was not affected that much.

Years later I read it again and was riveted. I guess I just wasn't ready to receive the information early on, even though I needed to learn every word of it. I have read it at least twice since then, plus many other great books on success, money, chiropractic, philosophy, and theology.

Saying to remember: *The first part of all you earn is yours to keep.*

Stated in affirmation form:

The first part of all I earn is mine to keep!

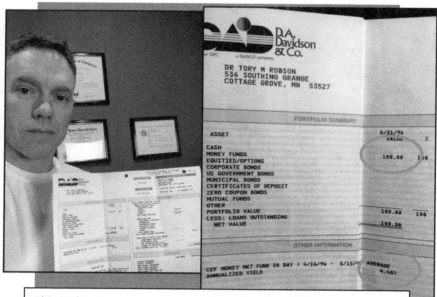

This is the statement I received from the first $100 I ever saved as a chiropractor. How I thought to save this back in 1996 is amazing. Notice circled also is what the Money Market interest rate was paying back then, 4.45!. At the time it was considered low. Today the Money Market interest rate is commonly .01%. This is 445% less than in 1996. While the interest <u>we get</u> dropped 445%, the interest <u>we pay</u> on mortgages only dropped 50%. What a rip!

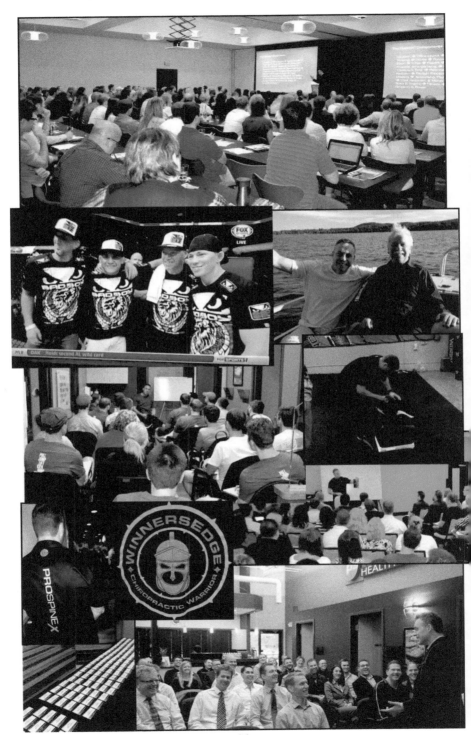

WINNERSEDGE
CHIROPRACTIC CONSULTING

When it's time to get serious about your practice and future success.

47

Q: Now What Are the Money Priorities of the Rich Chiropractor?

First let me say this. A few out there might want to oppose some of what I say and reply: *"It's not always about the money."*

Well let me clue you in, when you are 70 years old and sitting there with nothing saved and unable to earn much you will quickly say: *"Damn, it actually was about the money."* You cannot retire on patient visits. You will need real money. It's best for all chiropractors to understand this as early as possible.

Quotes by success legend Napoleon Hill from *The Laws of Success*.

- *"If you cannot develop the habit of saving money then the seeds of greatness aren't even in you."*

- *"No sacrifice is too great to avoid the misery of debt."*

- *"Those without money are at the mercy of those who have it."*

In coaching I see doctors doing $70,000 or more in monthly collections. Yet after 10 years in practice they are $20,000 behind on taxes, have 14 different debts, and less than $1000 saved. This is no joke. They think more money will fix their problems. Will it? Is the real problem their lack of discipline and faulty system?

A chiropractor in this situation may not see the debt for how evil it really is. Unless acted upon by a serious and influential outside source (power consultant like me) this chiropractor may be ruined permanently.

See, once this cycle starts, the man or woman normally can never get out from under the payments. They have created a mess due to their ignorance or sheer foolishness. They will need to change their unearned lifestyle back to what they can truly afford. This is not easy.

Correcting this deflates the chiropractor's ego back to reality. This really hurts and is difficult to endure temporarily. Going from the brand-new BMW to a used Camry, or from the fancy home you bragged about back into a small rental can hit the ego hard.

When a chiropractor decides to correct their money handling back to what it should have been all along they have to explain it all to a husband, wife, friends, neighbors, chiro friends, or whoever. It may not sound like fun, but it is very smart to go back to where you should have stayed until you could actually afford the life you attempted to buy.

A chiropractor who is backwards and upside down with money may even have relationship, staff, fitness, and practice troubles. These types of drama seem to go hand in hand with money mishandling.

Conversely, when a person is really good with money, it is amazing how many other things in their life just seem to excel. Want to become more attractive, feel better, and be ten times happier overnight? Get good at properly and smartly handling money!

People who are good with money earn a respect that is so palpable it is hard to describe. People just seem to move out of the way wherever they walk. Those that are not good with money get bumped into and have everyone making fun of them behind their back. Which one would you rather be?

Priorities, in order, of the RICH chiropractor:

1. Desire to bring increase to others.
2. Taxes are automatically paid immediately.
3. Payroll taxes automatically paid immediately.
4. All office and personal essentials paid automatically.
5. Giving automated to one or more worthy causes.
6. Debt elimination plan in place and rolling.
7. Saving automated.
8. Themselves.

Notice that the rich chiropractor puts personal expenses last with what is left. If nothing is left after all expenses this doctor still feels great. They know everything is current. Their debt is lowering, savings is growing, net worth is growing, and others are a little better from their generosity. It is very satisfying. It feels 100 times better than having a high stress, over financed, money treadmill lifestyle.

Notice how the system I describe automatically increases your net-worth every week without even trying. When a doctor's net worth grows it holds true that their self-worth grows right along with it. This system is also **scalable** for the chiropractor.

Q: What Do You Mean by Scalable?

Scalable for our purposes here means this: Will the doctor's money flow system blow apart if you start shoving more money into it? Where is it weak? At what point will it break down? When will it fail?

Notice the chiropractor whose habits and systems are upside down, if you add more money into their life with their weak habits, they will only go farther in the hole. They will buy more stuff for themselves and take on more expenses. They foolishly think the money will last forever only to realize they are more behind on taxes and paying debts.

More money means more responsibility. **If a person is not responsible with their current level of money what do you think will happen if they get more?**

A backwards, self-centered system and mindset is <u>not efficient and certainly not scalable.</u> Their situation and financial position actually goes farther backwards when more money is added.

Once again, understand this fact: More money only brings you more of what you <u>already have</u>.

Most are not experts with money and NEVER understand this. They cannot understand it because they are not smart enough yet. They always believe more money will fix their problems. Just like a gambler always feels the next hand or next roll will make them rich. It normally only ruins them on a larger scale.

Unless a doctor does some major and immediate mind re-programming, they will just be stressed and upside down on a bigger scale. Net worth tells an important story.

However, if you are crushing debt, saving, and giving, <u>then add more money</u> guess what happens? **You will be crushing debt even faster plus saving and giving even more because your system is scalable!**

- The winner always wants a better system. More money can and will flow into it.

- The loser just wants the money. This is why they are losing and always will until they get smarter.

- Every money level has its required system.

- You will only grow to your level of financial organization. Your system must be able to "scale up" as income increases.

- The smart steady tortoise always beats the flashy hare.

- Your self-image grows as your net worth grows. If your net worth is low, your self-image will be dragged down with it.

- Get your money flow fixed before the mess is too big to repair.

- Make friends with at least one really good money handler.

- If you can say: *"I can't afford that just yet"* you can be rich.

Who are you trying to impress anyway?

We all want to impress people. Everyone goes about doing this in a different way. I am suggesting here to <u>not do it</u> by financing things you cannot afford in order to try and be cool.

People try to "look richer" than they really are. It commonly manifests in the form of a lease on an entry level model luxury car like a BMW 3 series, Audi, or Mercedes etc. Be aware, those that really have the money and life you wish you had can easily see you are a poser.

We all care about other people's opinions. I certainly do. Really think about it, who would you rather be: The person who <u>is rich</u> and on their way or a broke chiropractor trying to look like it?

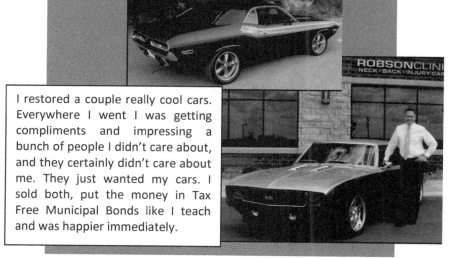

I restored a couple really cool cars. Everywhere I went I was getting compliments and impressing a bunch of people I didn't care about, and they certainly didn't care about me. They just wanted my cars. I sold both, put the money in Tax Free Municipal Bonds like I teach and was happier immediately.

The smart doctor doesn't have to try to look rich. He or she instead stays cool, hammers debt, attends more seminars, is conservative, saves religiously, and pays off all debt decades sooner than other DCs.

- Be the man or woman who people know is solid, credible, wise, and financially powerful. Be the mighty Oak that others look to.

- It is ok to have cool stuff, but <u>never</u> before taxes, giving, your debt plan, and savings are all handled.

- The cars I just showed you were paid for with cash. When the system is in order, you can do whatever you want with the money you have after all priorities are handled. A great feeling!

Q: What Are Some Good Resources to Learn More?

Books:

- *The Richest Man In Babylon* -George Clason
- *How To Really Ruin Your Financial Life* -Ben Stein
- *The Science Of Getting Rich* -Wallace Wattles
- *Stop Acting Rich* -Thomas Stanley
- *Book of Proverbs* -Old Testament

CD sets:

- *Prosperity Secrets For Chiropractors* -Robson
- *Prosperity Affirmations For Chiropractors* -Robson
- *How To Save Money Crush Debt And Become Financially Free For Chiropractors* -Robson
- *7 Pillars of Personal and Professional Success* -Robson

Videos:

- *WINNERSEDGE Business and Money Vids* Members Only
- *Money as Debt* YouTube
- *The American Dream* (30 min cartoon) YouTube
- *Wealth Seminar* -Dan Kennedy YouTube
- *You Were Born Rich* -Bob Proctor YouTube

Anything you see out there will make you realize just how good WINNERSEDGE material really is. It is real world specific for DCs.

Q: Okay Tory Let's Go Back to This, When Is It a Good Time To Buy A Home?

Here are a few rules I feel are worth considering.

Buy a home if:

- All small debt is paid.

- Student loans and all business debt are completely paid.

- Taxes, saving, and giving are all established.

- You know you are not going to want to move for a loooong time.

- You actually need a home.

- You actually want to own and care for a home.

- You can get a home that has the features you really want.

- Your practice is solid and will not need to re-locate or require any significant money or upgrades for some time.

- You can legitimately afford it, the phantom payments, and the lifestyle that comes with the level of home you choose.

Here is our guideline for how much home you can afford:

The total monthly payment including principal, interest, tax and insurance must be under 18% of the monthly gross profit for the household. Gross profit is the money you have after all legit business expenses are paid, but before your taxes are paid.

- If you collect $25,000 per month and your total overhead is $15,000 this leaves you $10,000. 10,000 x .18 = $1800 max you can afford in principal, interest, tax and insurance.

- If you collect $40,000 per month and your overhead is $25,000 this leaves you $15,000. 15,000 x .18 = $2700 max you can afford in principal, interest, tax and insurance.

- If you collect $75,000 and the overhead is $40,000 then you have $35,000 x .18 = $6300 max you can afford all in.

Some readers may have a spouse with contributory income and this must be considered. The key is **we never take on expenses that**

hurt or kill our ability to save. If the *Rapid Fire* is in order, taxes are perfect, and we are "saving our age" then you can do whatever you like with the rest of your money and not feel guilty.

Buy the right home at the right time. Once all the smoke clears and your money flow is reorganized and automated with all the new home expenses, you can move on to the next level.

The next level goal is to make the monthly house payment and add another weekly payment in addition. It does not matter what the amount is to start, just set it up and get it started!

Ultimately, the goal is to have a **full loan acceleration** on the home mortgage.

- A full loan acceleration is a double mortgage payment on a 30-year note. After this the interest savings diminishes.

- A full loan acceleration on a 15-year loan is a 1.5x payment.

    o **Example starting out:** Your mortgage is $2800 a month. You make the regular mortgage payment every month. You also set up an auto-payment of another $100 recurring every week.

    o **Example of a full loan acceleration**: Your mortgage is $2800 a month. You make the regular mortgage payment every month and also set up an auto-payment of another $700 recurring every week. (You are paying the regular $2800 plus another $2800 that is broken down into $700 payments every week.)

- We do this weekly because it ties in with how you get paid weekly. The faster the money gets to the debt the quicker it takes a bite out of the principal.

- Of course, make sure the extra you pay is going directly to principal.

- If you buy a home for $400,000, you will pay around $370,000 in interest for a total of $770,000. This does not include all the phantom payments along the way.

- If you pay just another $100 per month towards the principal you will save over $35,000 in interest!

- On a $400,000 home if you pay an extra $500 per month towards the principal you will save over $120,000 in interest.

- If you use what I teach and do a full loan acceleration you will save over $228,000 in interest and pay the loan off 20 years sooner!

- The more curious reader may wonder why I have not paid down the mortgage on the property shown earlier. The reason is because it is a rental. I am letting the tenant pay the mortgage. There is no reason for me to add extra money to it at this time. Extra cash can be better used elsewhere.

Q: What About Building a Home?

Building a home can be an incredible experience. I only recommend this for the very well organized and well financed chiropractor.

This is an entire lesson by itself. If any doctor wants to build a home I recommend they call me. In fact, before any chiropractor builds anything they should call me.

Q: A Minute Ago You Said "Save Your Age." What Does That Mean?

This is another incredibly smart and life changing concept we have at WINNERSEDGE. I have to say, the WINNERSEDGE chiropractor knows much more compared to other doctors when it comes to the key things that will really matter in the future.

This is why we call our seminar the *True Chiro Success Seminar* because we are completely concerned with what really makes a chiropractor successful in practice and in life.

I do not recall where in the past the "saving your age" idea came from. I think I may have heard it from an old consultant named Greg Stanley. I'm not sure where he learned it from, he has since retired from chiropractic consulting. I picked up on it and perpetuate its value. It is a very smart and mathematically sound standard.

Saving your age is simple to understand, but not so simple to do in real life. In my experience, maybe 10 chiropractors in 100 can ever do this with any long-term consistency. Decide to be one of them.

You take your age and multiply it by 1000. That is how much you should be saving every year. I would rather say you NEED to be saving. If you are not then hang with me and do everything I teach.

Examples:

- A 38-year-old doctor must be saving $731 after all tax and expenses every week automatically and never miss a payment. ($731 x 52 weeks = $38,000 saved per year.)

- A doctor who is 54 must be saving $54,000 every year. This is $1040 <u>every week</u> automatically after all taxes and expenses are covered, including any debt acceleration.

- Using this ingenious guideline, how much should **you** be saving every week right now? $_____

- How much are **you** actually auto-saving every week religiously right now? $_____

Remember, excuses are normally lies created to cover up the real truth. If you are not to this level of saving yet, just admit the real reason and get after it!

A couple reasons are: You did not know this guideline until now or you have not yet worked hard enough to become the productive and disciplined man or woman capable of creating and sustaining the type of practice collecting the money that will get you to this level.

Yes, I know, <u>everyone</u> will have some setbacks and crisis in their life. We all experience certain occurrences of tragedy. Everyone has these. You are not special. Past trauma must be used as success fuel.

<u>If a chiropractor can go to an office and care for patients, then they can be more successful</u>. It goes without saying that any situation in life is easier when you have more money. Money is a great comforter. Money gives choices. Money has the power to fix a lot of things in a hurry. I'd rather cry with $900,000 in the bank than with only $500.

Q: So What Do You Feel Is Required for a Chiropractor to Call Themselves "Successful?"

I want to be super clear. The goal is to:

1. Pay off all small debt.
2. Pay off all student loans.
3. All practice debt is gone.
4. All credit cards have zero balances.
5. Cars are paid for, or are being paid weekly as talked about.
6. Own a smart home with the regular payment plus another weekly payment until ultimately a double payment is being made
7. The doctor is <u>also</u> saving their age every year after tax. Automatically saved weekly of course, per our system.

Yes, <u>there are many levels of success in many areas of life.</u> Here we are talking financially. In consideration of this let's look at these general guidelines. **What level are you at right now?**

Level 1: Supporting self fully. The doctor is paying all bills and all debts with no help from mommy, daddy, hubby, wife, whoever, credit card, or any bank.

Level 2: Supporting self fully and has WINNERSEDGE money system architecture in place with small amounts.

Level 3: This doctor is eliminating small debts and rolling the "found money" into the *Rapid Fire.* This doctor has discipline and is gaining momentum and confidence.

Level 4: All small debt is gone. Now attacking student loans with a *Rapid Fire* of at least twice the monthly payment.

Level 5: Student loans are now gone. No small debt. No practice debt. No leases. Doctor at this level is now saving their age automatically. May also be saving for a home.

Level 6: DC buys a smart home. Accelerates the mortgage with a little extra. Still saving age automatically. Taxes are current and money flow system solidly in place.

Level 7:   The doctor is now doing a full loan acceleration on the home <u>and</u> is saving their age. Net worth is starting to grow with some velocity. Interest is being earned.

Level 8:   Home acceleration continues per plan, the chiropractor now hits their first $100,000 saved.

Level 9:   DC here is good at avoiding the countless scorpions and all their ideas on how you can lose your money. Doctor stays steady and now gets to $200,000 saved.

Level 10:   Home equity is significant, but of course there is no thought of touching it. Now has $500,000 safely put away in Tax Free Municipal Bonds like we recommend earning over $10,000 every 6 months in tax free interest. The WINNERS**EDGE** *Vortex Accelerated Saving System* is in full power.

Level 11:   Doctor becomes a net worth millionaire where their assets exceed their liabilities by one million dollars.

Level 12:   Savings now over $750,000. All else is in order. A true cash lifestyle is starting to emerge. Still avoiding stupid, overly complex, high commission, impossible to understand, and even more impossible to benefit from ideas being pitched like real estate, over funded whole life insurance policies, or other "investments" in things that even the person selling them doesn't understand. Doctor is becoming increasingly savvy and avoids things that make no <u>real</u> sense and add no <u>real</u> benefit to their life. Now saving over twice their age automatically ($1500 or more per week).

Level 13:   Doctor becomes a true Cash Millionaire. Practice is rolling great. DC is in great health and well conditioned from hard workouts. Home is updated as desired using cash. Buys whatever they want within reason for cash. Now earning over $44,000 a year in tax free interest. Now may be saving at least three times their age automatically ($3000+ every week.)

Level 14:   Doctor now has over $1.5 Mil saved. Sits very happy and realizes they did not need to try and do anything outside chiropractic to do well. Opportunities may arise. DC here is very careful and only considers investments that are in areas where they are an expert, take little time, and have a predicable low risk return. While everyone else has lost money, their satisfaction with modest and consistent returns works. Doctor here never puts more than 10% of anything at risk. Saving $4000 or $5000 automatically every week is possible. No need to ever save for things like college. Such expenses are just paid with cash when they arise.

Level 15: Home is now paid for, no debt anywhere except maybe on vehicles but by choice and not necessity. Two million+ put away earning $88,000 per year in tax free interest. Engineering transition out of practice, but no rush. Net worth well over $3,000,000.

Level 16: No debt unless for convenience. Their **Vortex Accelerated Saving System** is growing faster than they can spend it with their smart disciplines. Bond interest and/or asset revenue is now enough to cover all expenses easily without ever touching the principal. Income is still rolling in. Focus now shifts to philanthropy and how to get the money and assets transferred to heirs. Will and estate planning are priorities. This chiropractor truly "is rich" and can be considered "wealthy."

It does not require a huge practice or massive collections to get to this level. It just takes the planning and discipline to stay contained and not do dumb things. I coach chiropractors right now collecting $30,000 who will be much "richer" than doctors collecting $80,000 per month. Habits are what create wealth.

At seminars you might see chiropractors who look and talk like they have all the money, but 10 feet away sitting quietly will be a chiropractor who actually <u>does</u> have all the money.

I can go on, but you get the idea. Vacation homes, boats, other major expenses, supporting other family members who are not like you; there are countless other things that can be added in, but the core system is never altered! Tax, Debt, Save, and Give simultaneously.

Q: So How Do You Define "Wealth?"

Here is how I define wealth: *Wealth is how long you can go with a decent lifestyle if your income completely stopped.*

Really think about this. How long could you go? Right now you get no more collections, no more paycheck, and no more money put into any bank accounts. **How long could you survive before having to beg or borrow?** Is it a couple weeks? Is it a few months? Is it a few years? Is it many years? Is it your entire life?

I would call a person truly "wealthy" once they have enough built up to go the rest of their life without ever having to work again. Their assets are enough to cover all expenses and sustain them. The doctor can then pass this on to their family. If the heirs have smart money skills they will be in great financial shape, hopefully grow it, and pass it on themselves.

I am often amazed at how few people inherit any money these days. In all my 400,000 minutes on the phone with DCs so far, I can recall only 3 times a doctor inherited any money and the largest amount was $180,000. Of course I have suggestions on how to maximize this if a doctor is fortunate enough to have this happen. Be the person who leaves an inheritance!

Q: Why Do You Call Some People "Scorpions?"

There is a very powerful story I love to tell about a scorpion and a frog on the bank of a small meandering river. I will tell it to you later, but the moral to the story is this: **Everyone is out for their own benefit regardless of what they say or how they look on the surface.** Every week I am teaching doctors how to detect and dismiss any scorpions.

If you ask a wolf to watch your steaks while you are away of course he will say: *"I will be glad to look after them for you..."*

You must be able to spot the scorpions. They will not sound or appear like one. Learn from the Bible when it says: *"And no wonder, The Devil himself masquerades as an angel of light."*

Q: What Is a Tax Free Municipal Bond?

It is the foundational investment of choice for the chiropractor. This is my experienced opinion. They are pretty easy to explain, which is a good sign already. When a city needs money to build something expensive like a $12,000,000 water treatment plant, they don't have the money sitting there. They create and sell bonds.

They will need some financial house like Morgan Stanley, for example, to do it for them. They don't have the ability in their office to handle this. You and I can then buy some of the bonds. The bonds will then pay you a stated rate of interest like 4.4% <u>and</u> give you back your principal in a specified number of years. For example: 12 years.

The city just elevates the local taxes to get the money to pay you and everyone else back who bought some of their bonds. So the safety of bonds comes from the fact that the city has the power to collect taxes to pay you back. This is about as safe as an investment can get because taxes are not going anywhere. A city would have to go bankrupt to default on bonds. Of course, we would never buy bonds that were not attached to reliable and economically sound areas.

For example: Bonds sold to pay for an addition to the Las Vegas Airport would be smarter than bonds for a declining town near an old nuclear testing range.

Notice, <u>you are loaning money to the municipality.</u> You are a lender. If you do this in your own state the bonds are state and federal tax exempt. This is why they are called Tax Free Municipal Bonds.

Now listen carefully: In investing you only have two choices. You can either be an <u>owner</u> or a <u>lender</u>.

- An **Owner**: If you buy a company stock or a mutual fund full of stocks you are a little part owner of the companies in the portfolio. Guess what, stocks can and will go up or go down. <u>You have absolutely no control over it.</u> You can lose all your money in a day. It really is gambling, and not only that but you are usually letting someone else gamble your money for you. A double dose of insanity.

- A **Lender**: First observe that the richest people and institutions on the planet are lenders. They loan money to people and companies. There are even vastly wealthy families behind companies that lend their own money to entire Governments. The largest buildings in every city are what? Banks! Stadiums are named after what? Here in Minneapolis it is called *US Bank Stadium*. Learn from this and become a lender.

Bonds are not glamourous. Rarely will any broker know about them, talk about them, or sell them. They are low or no commission items. The broker can be a scorpion and try to steer you to buy what is best for them. Again, beware. There are few places that sell bonds with the criteria we teach. We have recommendations for our members.

After 20+ years now I still like them. They are hard to beat on sheer math, or behaviorally in the chiropractor's life. They are great for a doctor's overall financial plan.

A test: You have bought into an investment idea. I then ask you: *"Tell me how it all works."* If you have to refer me to someone else for an explanation, simply know you might have a problem.

Key points:

- Learn to be happy with modest and consistent returns.

- Be smart and avoid any "illusions of grandeur." Never think that you are different and that somehow you will be lucky in investing. Again, read the *Richest Man in Babylon* very slowly and pay attention.

- You would have to get over 10% in stocks to match 4.4% in bonds. Why? Commissions, fees, and taxes eat the 10% down to less than 5% if you are lucky.

- Even the stock wizards in history, like Peter Lynch in his book *One Up on Wall Street*, conclude that the best investor experts in history cannot do better than 10% over time.

- As chiropractors, our income is good enough that we do not have to try to get investments to return unreasonable amounts.

- If an investment keeps track with inflation this is excellent.

- To get a small yield increase in an investment brings a HUGE and disproportionate amount of risk. If you want to get a 1% increase in yield, the risk can be 10 times greater. Not worth it.

- We never put our retirement money at risk. We have worked way too hard for it!

- There is **saving** money. There is **investing**. There is **speculating**. Today what people call saving is actually speculating and risky. If it can go down it is speculating. Please no speculating with more than 10% of your money.

- Remember the most valuable thing you can do is take care of patients. Wasting any time on investing or other such agendas is not necessary. Work to help people, earn money, pay debt, buy safe investments consistently, and you will win.

- The doctor who tries to make it big or becomes a part time real estate investor, or day trader, or anything else will virtually never beat the doctor who is focused, stays cool, and stays the course.

- You can get paid $40 per minute as a chiropractor. What are you EVER going to do that will be better than this?

- Dedicate all time and effort to getting good and seeing more people. This is by FAR the most profitable use of your time. Then invest in smart and low stress investments that make sense.

- Remember, the easiest way to earn more as a chiropractor is to see more people. Never by taking time away from practice to mess with other things you are not an expert in.

- Many chiropractors would have been better off to put money in a mattress. Doctors lose money like crazy. Other professionals too, for that matter. Don't lose your money. **Hold on to your money.** "Preserve principal" it is called.

- Again, if you are not <u>empowered</u> in handling money you will be <u>overpowered</u>. (By a scorpion most likely.) They win and you lose. My Dobermans can sniff out a scorpion from 20 feet away.

- Being smart, cool, surefooted, and steady are the keys to really serious success.

- Simplicity is key. Once you start to get overly complex in any area just know you are probably off track.

- Make money, pay debt, buy bonds, sleep well. Easy.

- 401ks, SEPs, Roths, Profit Sharing and other Pre-tax vehicles are expensive and complex. I see little if any use for these for a DC.

- The worst is when a friend or family member is in the "investing" world and tries to be your guide. You don't need them. I wouldn't listen to anyone who is not richer than me.

- Never be impressed by people in fancy suits, fancy offices with elevators, or with computers that have lots of numbers running across the screen. This is all just a show.

- Never be impressed by anything you see like fancy cars, watches or other displays of money. Only be impressed by real money.

- Never feel inferior or that you are not as smart as others when it comes to money. If you understand this booklet you will know more relevant and useful principles than practically anyone you ever meet. Regardless of appearances.

- Becoming rich is a $100 bill at a time boring process. Key word is **process**. Embrace this.

- Yes, there are some who started 30 years before you and have done well in things like real estate or other non-chiropractic endeavors. Never think you can duplicate another person's success in an area where you are not an expert. The time to become an expert elsewhere is littered with huge losses and a TON of lost money from what you are already an expert at. Do what you are supposed to be doing and that is adjusting patients.

- Never be fooled by big numbers being thrown around on TV or elsewhere. Always acknowledge the fact that it is a big deal to save $1 Million dollars as a chiropractor. Generally, it is saving $20,000 a year for 50 years in a row. Or saving $50,000 a year for 20 years in a row. Or saving $1000 every week, after tax, for over 1000 weeks straight. This is serious.

- Again, the real goal here is to keep your money and not lose it. You traded part of your life for it.

- Understand how EVIL and life destroying debt really is. Never let its commonness fool you. It is common, but it is not normal! Like headaches. They are common, but never normal.

- The 4 Ds are what we must avoid in any way we might have the power to do so: Death, Disability, Debt and Divorce.

Q: What Do You Mean by *Vortex Accelerated Savings System?*

This is another one of my named concepts. Follow this: You start saving until you have enough to buy a bond. The bond interest is now going into your account. You become a better chiropractor and are able to save even more money. With your accelerated savings and the bond interest you're now earning, you then buy another bond. Now you have two bonds earning interest. That money is going into your account plus what you are saving. You then are able to pile up money faster so you can buy another bond even sooner. Now it also is paying you interest with the other bonds you have, plus you are still saving so you can buy another interest paying bond sooner yet. Get the idea?

In this case I call it *"Becoming a bond collector."* Observe how the amount you accumulate starts to increase at an increasing rate. I named this the **Vortex Accelerated Saving System.**

When executed perfectly over time it will get you to the point where your interest alone will cover all your monthly bills. At this point you have officially won the game.

I want you to really think about what I just said. Do you see how smart this is? Have you ever in your life been shown any workable plan to saving and accumulating money before you read this? What is this booklet really worth?

Of course, for my clients we draw it all out and create the detailed flow and plan for them specifically. We call this the *Cash Flow* diagram for the chiropractor. It is nice to see the flow visually.

You might be thinking I am just some chiro money guy. <u>I am not just some chiropractic financial guy</u>. I am a serious chiropractor first and am the full-on everything consultant. There is nothing whatsoever as it relates to taking a dirt hillside, designing and building a chiropractic office, staffing it, adding all the procedures, marketing, to everything required to take it over $1,000,000+ a year in collections that I would not be considered one of the world's foremost experts at.

I have made money from practice and from consulting. I have made a decision to work to become good at handling it. This booklet is simply a few chapters from the Tory Robson chiropractic success information playbook.

Now just for fun read this:

GETTING RICH.

not plenty of money can have all he
wants. Life has advanced so far, and
become so complex, that even the most
ordinary man or woman requires a
great amount of wealth in order to
live in a manner that even approaches
completeness. Every person naturally
wants to become all that he is capable
of becoming; this desire to realize innate possibilities is inherent in human
nature; we cannot help wanting to be
all that we can be. Success in life is
becoming what you want to be; you can
become what you want to be only by
making use of things, and you can have
the free use of things only as you become rich enough to buy them. To
understand the science of getting rich
is the

The above is a page from *The Science of Getting Rich* by
Wallace Wattles in 1912. What do you think of these
words? Are they true? He goes on to say:

> *"The desire for riches is really the desire for a fuller
> more abundant life; and that desire is praiseworthy. The
> person who does not desire to live more abundantly is
> abnormal, and so a person who does not desire to have
> money enough to buy all they want is abnormal."*

What do you think about these words? *Are they true?*
They are absolutely true. These words could hurt a few
people's feelings. Some will deny anything that exposes
their inability to make more out of their lives. A few will
even try to say: *"Money can't buy you love."* This is
absolutely false. A high quality person with a little money
will have no lack of opportunities for friends of all kinds.
Scorpions exist in the relationship world too, so beware.

Q: Tory, Do You Ever Have Doctors Say They Are "Burned Out?"

Yep. After I stop laughing I go to work on them. *"Burned out?"* On what? Delivering the most amazing and honest service to humanity using only your bare hands, with a schedule that you get to control, in an office that you own, for an incredibly fair fee, giving adjustments that have the power to completely transform the lives of everyone they touch? Not to mention you can get paid more than enough to create an incredible life for you and those you care about.

Why were you so *"burned out"* again? Most of these doctors should be slapped back to attention. As Demartini might say: *"These chiropractors suffer from digito-oral-cranio-rectalitis."* In other words, they are sucking their thumb and have their head up their ass at the same time. If they had a glass belly button you could wave at them.

It is worth noting here that most DCs who call me saying they are "burned out" are really saying: *"I have messed up and now I sit here with very little to show for my years of work. I have less energy to go for growth. I want insurance companies and patients to just pay me more for doing less. I see the years ticking by and I am mad at myself because looking back if I had just been smarter I'd be a lot better off right now."*

They don't have as much money as they think they should considering how hard they've worked for so many years. What a horrible feeling.

In reality, this means they had no money flow system, no good coaching, and who knows what else that needs to be fixed. They sometimes have let millions pass through their hands with little or nothing to show for it now. Burnout comes from unrewarded work.

There can be divorces, health issues, family events, bankruptcies, natural disasters, an attack by killer bees, you name it, but that is all in the past. Give thanks, forgive, and roll on. Why? Because that is what a winner always does. <u>A winner always learns and rolls on to success.</u>

Key phrase to say: *I'm sorry, please forgive me, I forgive you, I thank you, I love you.* This phrase is incredibly powerful.

Some are saying they are burned out when they are actually just bored. A bored chiropractor can be one who has done very well financially and seeks a new challenge.

67

Who are these pictures of?

Is it a stressed out chiropractor? One who did not pay the price to learn how to become a successful man or woman? One who made mistakes and never fixed them?

Is it a chiropractor who thought there was an easier way and got off track?

Is it a chiropractor who is upside down with their money and has yet to learn how to handle money correctly?

Is it a chiropractor who failed to listen to those smarter than them, and instead wanted to do things "their way?"

Is it a person who had a divorce, famly crisis, health issue or other life event and let it "ruin them?" Then dragged it out instead of working past it to become successful?

Is it a chiropractor who is all mad, stressed, and anxious because they never learned how to forgive or be thankful?

Is it the crybaby "burned-out" chiropractor who has lost value for all the incredible things in their life?

Is it the chiropractor who has yet to start paying down debt?

Is it the DC in trouble because they can't follow the laws?

It's actually Sisyphus of Greek mythology, who was punished for his self aggrandizing craftiness and deceitfulness by having to roll an immense boulder up a hill, only to watch it roll back down, repeating this action for eternity.

Burnout and countless other things that divert the chiropractor off-mission can all be righted fairly quickly, but only if the chiropractor is teachable and still has a little fire left in them.

Vince Lombardi says: *"You'd be surprised how much confidence a little success will bring."*

You see, I am not in the consulting business. I am actually in the <u>freedom</u> business. Health + Time + Money = Freedom!

Q: What Else About Money?

As a chiropractor continues to mature he or she will see the reality of how money works, and that the way to success in chiropractic is with small amounts over time. We call it the WINNERSEDGE "small amounts weekly" concept.

The doctor totally forgets, and now laughs at the "someday I will make it big" concept that some are still hanging onto. Some doctors spend their entire career trying to find the home run, the next big thing, the next tool, marketing angle, or whatever that will make money fall from the sky.

The smarter chiropractor just rolls along steady and smart. One day at a time, one week at a time, and one dollar at a time. Years later there is no catching this chiropractor because the "searching" doctor can never make up for the lost time.

A few HUGE landmarks. A lot of good happens from this point. These prove the correct habits are now being established:

1. All small debt is paid.
2. All practice debt is paid.
3. Student Loans are paid in full.
4. Doctor gets to saving their age.
5. Doctor saves up their first $100,000.

The chiropractor also learns to avoid hobbies that eat money like crazy until they can actually afford them: Powerboat racing, Rolex collecting, antique car restoring, and excessive golf, just to name a few.

Along the way every chiropractor will learn facts that can and will burst illusions. Facts that may seem disappointing initially but are actually liberating once understood.

Q: What Do You Mean "Burst Illusions?"

Let me explain: For a chiropractor to take home $250,000 they must collect $1,000,000. The illusion occurs when a doctor has "thought" their collections = their income. *Wrong!*

- Reality: A doctor's income is what is left <u>after</u> all overhead expenses and all taxes are fully paid. Then all personal expenses come out of that.

- A doctor collects $250,000 – overhead and taxes = at most $75,000 a year = a net income of $6,250 per month.

- A doctor collects $400,000 – overhead and taxes = at most $120,000 a year = a net income of $10,000 per month.

- Doctor collects $750,000 – overhead and taxes = at most $225,000 a year or maybe $18,000 per month net income.

This sometimes causes a "let down" in the doctor because they had some "illusions of grandeur" and visions of bigger numbers in their head. <u>They never really understood how money really works</u> in their business.

We must be able to distinguish between **total collections** and the **gross income** after all relevant clinic expenses. Then we must deduct the tax, leaving us with our **net income**. From this, all personal expenses are paid, leaving **disposable income**.

So:

1. Total collections – Clinic expenses = **Gross income**

2. Gross income – all Taxes = **Net income**

3. Net income – Personal expenses = **Disposable income**

The upside down doctor errantly thinks that their collections is their money. They think if they collect $500,000 a year that they "make $500,000 a year." *Wrong.*

They then spend more than what their actual disposable income is, leaving them unable to cover all the business expenses.

The smart doctor pays everything in order as shown earlier. The taxes are paid, office expenses are covered, then the personal expenses are made leaving some disposable income to enjoy guilt free.

It is a good time to note again that it is critical to KEEP EVERYTHING separate. NEVER spend clinic money on personal expenses. Every night there are television shows about people who spent the business-owned money on their personal life. It turns out bad.

Leave all business debit cards and credit cards in a drawer at the office. The real PRO only uses them for relevant business expenses.

Now back to a few examples:

- A doctor who is collecting $350,000 a year says: *"Before too long I will be saving $5000 per week!"* Oh really? Does this doctor know that to save $5000 per week as a chiropractor you have to collect around $1,500,000 a year? This is a long way from $350,000.

  o $1,500,000 – overhead and taxes = $450,000. Then you might be able to save the $260,000 a year ($5000 x 52) and even then you'd have to save 60% of your income.

  o The money ignorant would say: *"No problem, that would be easy with all that money."* The ignorant critic here fails to understand the expenses and lifestyle costs associated with that income level.

  o If any person can consistently save over 20% of their net income we call this excellent and quite rare.

- A very unique and successful person worked incredibly hard to grow their business and was able to save over $70,000 in one month after tax. Another guy who knew this person was pretty successful, upon hearing this says with seriousness: *Is that all?*

  o The critic here has never saved this much in a year, let alone in a month, yet has that comment. Why?

  o The total lack of understanding of the real dollar amounts involved at different levels. He should have fallen over at how incredible it was what he'd just heard.

- A person at a certain money level cannot wrap their mind around any money level above their own. **This means you.**

- Another example: A new doctor joins WINNERSEDGE and very seriously sets a collection goal for their first year at $1,000,000. The doctor argues with me when I suggest making it more reasonable and accurate. Four years later the doctor has yet to break $300,000. The "dream bubble" has burst. Now that this doctor's brain is back in reality we can get to growing!

The high-level chiropractor gets real with money and really works to understand it. The doctor who knows their numbers the best has the best chance for growth. We must accurately assess what is going on in all financial situations. What are the real costs, what are the taxes, what is left over, and what is smart to do with the money at that point.

A favorite is when a patient comes in, sees a bunch of other patients in the office and says to me: *"Yeah, looks like you are doing pretty well here huh Doc? This place is like an assembly line."* I love responding with: *"Yep, we help a lot of people here, everyone keeps sending in all their family and friends, but we always have room to take care of more people. Isn't chiropractic amazing? Who do you know that should be in here?"*

Remember, we don't answer questions, we "handle questions." The more successful you become, the fewer people will be able to relate to you. That is why you must have a coach like me who understands.

Q: What About CAs?

Example: You have a CA who thinks she works as hard as you and feels she should suddenly get an automatic $50,000 a year salary plus a bonus of 10% of the total collections or some other insane request.

Let's see: Their name is not on the lease. They do not have their name on all the debt. They are not the one who will get sued if anything happens (including if you get sued from something that they screwed up). They bring in none of the business. They are not the one that has the state Board looking over their shoulder. They are not the one delivering the care that requires a malpractice insurance policy. **They did not sacrifice the years and huge expense** of advanced schooling.

See once again, people just don't know how the math really works. As far as my opinion goes, the best CA on earth can get to $20 per hour and a bonus of 1% of monthly collections.

When a CA feels she is too good for the office it is time for her to go. One time I fired three staff members all in the same meeting. We then grew and broke all collection records within 6 months.

Key quote: *"Most people think they need a lot more money than they really do, then settle for a lot less."* -Earl Nightingale

Q: Do You Have Any Other Management Advice?

Many doctors actually have a CA, a spouse, even a kid, or their patients running their practice. Look carefully and you will see this is true. Very few doctors are actually running their own practice. Someone around them is making the decisions that are controlling what the doctor does and when it is done. This is so subtle in how it occurs.

- **Example**: A chiropractor complains that his afternoons are not as busy as they used to be and that something must be wrong. After really digging I discover his main CA asked if she could be done at 3:00 every day. He agreed since she had been such a great employee. He then goes and hires two part-time CAs for the afternoon. It really is not working as well as it should and the numbers show it.

  Question: Who is running his practice?

  Answer: Is it the CA? Or is it someone else? The CA has a kid she now wants to be with after school every day. So actually, the CAs kid is running this doctor's practice!

She wanted to be off at 3:00 more than he wanted to continue to grow. So her intention overpowered his. She got him to bend to her and now here I am as the coach left to engineer a solution to fix it.

Of course the solution is for the chiropractor here to wake up. be the boss on a mission, and not be so easily derailed. Practice success has requirements, not optional stuff but absolute requirements. One of those requirements is that we don't let CAs, CAs' kids, our own kids, parents, patients or whoever push us around and run our office.

Another problem: When a struggling DC has a "smart" spouse or parent who feels the DC "doesn't need coaching." I just shake my head.

There are endless examples of weakness where a strong doctor drifted off-mission. The doctor "on mission" will never tolerate any variation from what is needed to get the job done and serve the masses at a superior level. **There is one option and one option only.**

The most successful offices I have ever owned, consulted, and seen were all run by a doctor and a CA team where the DC and the main CA are ALWAYS there together every minute the clinic is open. Just like pilot and copilot. The synchronization, teamwork, and synergy created by this duo is a real secret to high level practice success.

Everyone else in the office orbits around this core pair. Cross training and the great weekly team meeting using the WINNERSEDGE agenda are needed so that everyone knows how to do everything well.

It is a bad mistake when only one CA knows how to do everything. This can leave the doctor vulnerable.

Q: Can You Talk About Taxes and Overhead?

Good news! By crushing debt you can dramatically lower your overhead percentage and even do better than the examples earlier. Yes you will pay more tax as your income goes up but who cares. You now have more money! Notice I said overhead percentage.

It is important right now to drill into your mind that **you WANT to pay more taxes.** Of course take every legal deduction you are allowed, but ultimately you want your taxes to increase, even double or triple. This means your income has increased dramatically.

Many people and doctors alike shun and complain about taxes. What these doctors are actually mad at is themselves for their lack of discipline. They have a weak system and are always behind on them. Even the smallest tax bill makes a doctor mad if they are behind because they spent the money on something else, when they should have paid their taxes FIRST.

- Key point: **You NEED to pay your taxes first. Of course you don't want to, but you NEED to pay the taxes first. If you don't, believe me...** *you will pay.*

- **The poor chiropractor** is always wound-up and stressed about their taxes and is commonly behind on them.

- The poor chiropractor has no idea they are totally destroying any chance of practice growth. Since they hate taxes, without even realizing it, they hate making more income.

- You cannot love making more money yet hate paying taxes. They are connected. No more denial. Simply accept that taxes are a part of business. Be happy with the part you get to keep because it could be a LOT worse.

- **Example**: One time before installing my first digital machine I was buying x-ray film. I hated paying the bill every month for x-ray film. I thought it was too high. Then I woke up and yanked my head out of my tail and realized that I actually wanted my x-ray film bill to double or triple. Why? Because that meant I had doubled or tripled my number of new patients.

- How could I want more new patients, yet hate paying for x-ray film at the same time? Do you get the idea?

- **The rich chiropractor,** on the other hand, pays their taxes weekly using the WINNERSEDGE system, never really thinks about them, and hums along focused on getting better as a chiropractor. This doctor adjusts their tax payments as needed months ahead of time if the practice and income grow. This doctor is relaxed, loves life, and naturally pulls more new ones.

- The rich chiropractor makes it look easy and wants to increase all expenses that are tied to growth. Unlike the poor chiropractor who always wants their overhead to go down, the rich DC has no issue with their overhead going up. The doctor wants their collection percentage to go down. This then makes their profit go up, which is the number that COUNTS.

- Doctors everywhere are always talking about collections when the number that really counts is net profit. This is what you can actually spend. You cannot spend "collections." Net profit is the only thing you can actually use and spend in your personal life.

Here are a few questions:

1. Is it possible to have great collections and no profit?

2. Is it true that some doctors who want to "lower their overhead" actually need their overhead to <u>go up</u> instead?

3. Is it true that a doctor can collect $20,000 per month and become rich, while a doctor collecting $80,000 per month is broke and in serious trouble?

4. Can you see how we NEVER want to cut expenses that are directly related and necessary to grow?

Examples:

A two DC office with one CA calls and says: *"Hey Tory, I want to talk about how we can lower our overhead."*

What is the correct answer? *"If you want to see more people and increase collections then you need your overhead to go up significantly. Starting with another CA since a two doctor office is crippled quickly with only one CA."*

A newer DC collecting $10,000 per month calls up and says: *"Hey Tory, can you look at my expenses and see where I can cut some overhead?"*

What's the answer? *"Dr. Trusty, what you need to do is focus on production and volume and collections. Ignore the overhead for now."*

A cranking DC collecting $90,000 per month calls and says: *"Hey Tory, you are the guru, answer me this: Why is it that every time I collect more, my overhead seems to follow it? When does it ever happen where you collect $90,000 with an overhead of just $15,000 or $20,000 instead of the normal $45,000 or more?"*

What's the answer? *Dr. Awesome, overhead always follows production as there are phantom payments in practice also. They are hard to describe and quantify, but to collect more money takes a little more of everything and that adds to overhead. Read my keys to overhead below and get after it!"*

Secrets to Low Overhead:

1. <u>Low debt</u> + low rent + correct staff + production = low overhead.

2. Increase production. Hit the streets and promote yourself and your office a LOT more. Double the people you know = double your practice.

3. Become a better skilled chiropractor. Get better!

4. Increase your earning potential via coaching and training.

5. Understand in the *Science of Getting Rich* when he says to do things in a "Certain way." That way is <u>efficiently</u>.

6. Efficiency of thought and action is the real secret to becoming rich. The seriously successful chiropractor is very good at knowing when they are not being time and money efficient and correcting it.

7. Live lean and be happy with cheap fun. Rent a canoe vs. buy a $200,000 twin engine luxury boat.

8. Debt = overhead. When you pay off debt you will be amazed how much extra money you will have.

9. Only have the staff you need. A doctor seeing 150 visits a week never needs 3 CAs. We have DCs seeing 150 in an afternoon with one CA. The Rule is: 1 CA per 40-50 visits a day.

10. Sometimes a doctor's overhead needs to <u>go up.</u> Have the courage to add expenses that will cause growth. Like coaching.

11. Get your mind on growing vs. trying to "cut costs."

12. Remember, if you have a "cut costs" and cheap mindset you can never prosper. **Prosperity can only come from a prosperity mindset.** Cheap people can rarely see their own poverty mindedness. Like people who smell can never smell themselves.

13. Yes, be conscious of all expenses, but never eliminate anything that is required to grow and serve more people.

14. Read every EOB, bill, agreement, and contract carefully. Be very organized with all business, money <u>inflow and money outflow</u>.

15. Have $1000 deductibles on auto policies.

16. Get the best space for the best price!

My new office where I still see patients and do all my consulting. We also hold many of our high level chiropractic training events here. Designed specifically for training chiropractors to be the best who ever lived in their area, we are quite certain that no consultant ever in history has had a place like this, with a purpose like this.

Those who are members of the WINNER**SEDGE** chiropractic success machine might already know this, but others reading may not. My new 1800 sq. foot office for my clinic and consulting is part of an 11,000+ sq. foot fitness center. I call it the WINNER**SEDGE Chiropractic Training Center**.

I have engineered the layout for the future with built in flexibility and I'm quite happy with it. Considering I design new offices all the time for chiropractors, and re-design horribly designed offices every week, this is a big statement.

The floorplan of a chiropractic office is what controls the flow in the office → the flow in the office determines how many people you can see in a day → which then determines how much you collect → which then determines your income → which then controls your life.

Your office design and layout have major control over your entire life. Floorplan design and office flow is a subject for another time. With my experience in construction, design, and architecture I feel our designs are the best that exist in chiropractic today. I can turn pretty much any space into a result seeking chiropractic success machine.

Now here's the point so listen carefully:

I engineered a deal with the gym owner where I pay no rent for 10 years. I pay no CAM, no Tax, no anything for 10 years. And, my name is not on any lease either.

Did you hear what I just said?

I was paying $4300 per month at my last space. The agreement I engineered for my new office is now saving me $516,000 and lowering my overhead by $4300 a month for the next 120 months.

It would take some time to explain how this was done. Several factors had to come together at the same time and place.

How to pay less, half, or no rent like myself is a subject for our private clients as they start out, or when their current leases near an end. It is not an easy thing to do, but it can be done as I have proven.

- Yes, overhead can get very low. Under 20% and even as low as 10% like I have been able to reach. This takes extremely good management, engineering, exactly the right situation, staffing, and serious efficiency coupled with BIG production.

- I see offices with 1 doctor and 2 CAs generating $20,000 per month of profit. I also see offices with 3 doctors and 11 staff generating just $5000 of profit per month for the DC owner.

- Beware of spending too much on advertising and marketing. These usually are not recommended until many other things that cost nothing are fixed. It is amazing the number of simple and free things you can do that will cause a practice to grow.

79

- So many doctors are wasting money on "marketing" when they have at least ten other things messed up which when fixed would launch them. I have so many examples and stories of this that would be incredibly valuable for you to hear.

- **Story**: A comedian is not very funny. He just cannot seem to get many people to pay and watch him perform. He calls me and says: *"Hey Tory, I think I need to do some advertising to get more people to come listen to me."* Will this work? Is a lack of advertising his problem? Of course not. This comedian just needs to be funnier. If the comedian is really funny, word will spread fast and his shows will sell-out. Chiropractic works the same way.

Key Quote: *"The first step in marketing a service, is the service itself."* -Harry Beckwith *Selling the Invisible*

- A chiropractor who is not seeing as many people as she would like, and keeping them for as long as she would like, calls me and says: *"Hey Tory, I think I need to do more advertising to get more new ones in here, can you help me?"*

  o What's the problem here? A lot. We install the WINNERSEDGE Report and Care Plans, killer Re-sign procedure, and Wellness plans. This doctors PVA elevates 20 more visits. She grows 100 more patient visits a week within 60 days and scraps all paid "advertising" forever.

- A chiropractor who is upside down, stressed out, takes 10-15 minutes per patient, is seeing around 100 a week and has for 18 years calls and says: *"Hey Tory, I want to grow to 200 a week and I'm doing all this advertising but it really isn't working, do you have something better I can try? Maybe Facebook ads or something?"*

  o What is the problem here? I show him how to fix his money flow, get his treatment time to under 5 minutes, and without a penny spent on "advertising" he rolls over 200 a week for the first time in his practicing life. He was then able to pay off $80,000 worth of debt that year.

- If a second CA is needed at around 40-50 visits per day, this will add significant overhead. This will also allow a practice to get over 200 a week. Ultimately the overhead percentage will decrease since there is more profit.
  - Before adding the 2nd CA:
    - Total overhead: $22,000 per month.
    - Total collections: $40,000 per month.
    - Overhead % is: 22,000/40,000 = 55%

- Cost of new CA is $2500 per month. Other elements of overhead also go up as a practice grows, but as a result of being willing to tackle the additional overhead FIRST let's see what happens:
  - After the 2nd CA starts:
    - Total new overhead: $26,000 per month.
    - Total collections: $50,000 per month.
    - Overhead % is: 26,000/50,000 = 52%
  - The collections then grow by $10,000 per month. $10,000 − $4000 in additional overhead = $6000 in net practice increase. Well done!

- The key for you is to pay off all debt, keep your taxes in order, make sure you have the best space for the best deal, keep yourself in great physical condition, and only have the staff you need to easily see the volume you desire. Then continue to get really good at EVERTHING!

Q: Any Other Tips on Taxes or Expenses?

Once you have a system in place and your taxes are current every week, we can get down to some serious production and prosperity.

Remember, the taxes you pay are a perfect reflection of what you earn, so remember, if you hate taxes you actually hate earning more.

We LOVE to earn more so we accept the taxes and have a system for them.

I will say here that any doctor who is thinking of some elaborate way to not pay taxes, or avoid payroll taxes is doomed. I just heard of a chiropractor who is headed to jail for not paying payroll taxes.

Interestingly, high volume chiropractors call me for advice on many things. They are often part of another group with a system which thinks more volume can fix everything. They are usually seeing 500 to 1000 visits a week and are working like dogs but not <u>taking home much real money</u>. Yet everywhere they go they brag about their volume.

Yes we want to see and help a lot of people, but not for free. They think if they can just get more new ones into their report and grow another 100 or 200 visits a week that it will fix everything.

Doctors in this system find themselves in a state of "living and dying by the prepay." Many don't realize how it even happened, or that there is any other way to practice.

They do tons of marketing → to get people into their big report → where they say anything they can to get people to start and prepay → so they can pay their bills → repeat.

They then feel trapped. It is like being on a treadmill and thinking that if you just run faster everything will get easier.

Volume and new patients are not always the solution. What these doctors need is a better, easier, more sustainable system. They also need a better schedule and patient payment arrangements which will then stabilize their weekly routine and cash flow.

Our system is so much better. Many times, these doctors are corrupted and have deeply ingrained bad habits from their past training. They cannot get themselves to join with me no matter how much truth, or how many facts, testimonials, or smart diagrams I throw at them.

"Yeah, you see 700 a week but Dr. Cool down the street <u>collects twice as much as you</u> working just 4 days a week loving life. You are plugging 6 days a week plus screenings on top of that and hating it."

We do not start self-limiting or dead-end procedures. These are procedures we are just going to want to quit doing anyway. If it is not something you can see adding into a system for a long time then reconsider.

There is an important saying you will hear, another Torysim if you will: ***"Money reaches farther than your hands."***

PERSONAL BESTS

Patients in one day 180	Goal 450-500	
Collections in one day $ 20,000	Goal 30K	
Visits in a week 576	Goal 1000-1500+	
Collections in a week $ 40K	Goal AVG 25K+	
Collections in a month $ 70K	Goal $ 100K	
Collections in year $ 527K	Goal 1 MILLION	
New Patients in a week 35	Goal 30	
New Patients in a month 65	Goal 100+	

I think I need the most help with:

☐ Treatment Time   ☑ Business
☐ Confidence   ☑ Promoting
☑ Money Handling   ☐ Goal setting
☑ Getting New Patients   ☐ Retention
☐ Staff Issues   ☐ Organization
☑ Increasing Income   ☑ Saving Money
☐ Debt Reduction   ☑ Time Management
☐ Insurance Billing   ☑ PI Building
☐ Cash Practice   ☐ Elevating Image

Other_____

GOALS

What 3 main things do you want to see change?

1. New patients ↑
2. Collections ↑
3. More time with my Family

Are you aware that YOU might be the problem? Yes

Are you willing to do what it takes to improve? Yes

I want you to really understand this so follow me closely.

Above is the Eval sheet we have DCs complete if they are interested in qualifying for WINNER**EDGE**. Look at it carefully.

- This doctor wants more family time and thinks that going from 500 a week to 1000 – 1500 visits a week will bring this?

- At 500 visits a week he complains that his collections need to go up?

- This doctor is collecting $23 per visit and thinks his biggest problem is that he needs more new patients?

- He is seeing 500 a week and only getting paid for maybe 200 of them. Now he wants to see 1000+ a week? With his system he will only get paid for maybe 500 of them and the other 500 will be free.

- Notice at the top right he has no idea what a debt plan is?

- See at the bottom he understands he is the problem.

- He also marks that he will do what it takes to improve.

Now <u>you be the consultant</u>. What is the real problem here?

1. Dump your current coach, scrap your outdated, volume chasing, and life destroying system, join WINNER**EDGE,** and pay attention.

2. Put WINNER**EDGE** money flow system in place. (Will fix $$)

3. Put WINNER**EDGE** Report , Pmts, OV, RE, and RS system in place.

4. Put WINNER**EDGE** weekly hours in place. (Will fix family time.)

This guy didn't qualify to join. His brain is so committed to an illusion he cannot grasp reality. Sad since I have the exact solution for him.

The more I do this the more it becomes clear that the **WINNERSEDGE** chiropractor is destined to be incredibly successful. Why? The **WINNERSEDGE** chiropractor has superior information and systems in the areas that actually count in practice and in life.

Now back to expenses:

The successful chiropractor and businessperson keeps track of average collections per visit and guards against going too far the wrong way. Anything under $30 per visit is in the danger zone.

The maturing doctor sees the reality of money. What really is due, what things really cost, what is really left over, then makes smart moves. Know that everything costs at least twice what you think, and that you always end up with less than you thought you were going to get. Combine these and you will rarely find yourself in trouble.

The "them them them" attitude must become solid. Doctors who are perennial powerhouses realize that they have nothing without patients and their team. They graduate past "self" to a much more genuine concern for "others." It becomes obvious and impressive.

- Each dollar you save is a soldier for you that earns more for you. Build an army!

- The more successful you get the more important having a coach becomes. *Lesser DCs fail to see this fact, flatline, even start "drifting" and predictably never reach their potential.*

- Lesser doctors will errantly see things that make them money as "costs" and shoot themselves in the foot. The typical **WINNERSEDGE** client makes $50,000 to $250,000+ more their first year as a member.

- We have never seen a doctor leave the group and do better than they did their last 12 months here. What a tragic mental error to make. Why anyone would quit the very thing that made and keeps them more successful is a mystery to me.

- Some just don't want to have more money and life. They can't mentally handle the responsibility that comes with it I guess.

- Another reason why coaching is automatic for the high level doctor is because coaching expenses are 100% tax deductible. Even the Government thinks chiropractors should have a coach.

- Example: A doctor is in a coaching program and grows massively. After a couple years they are only paying $500 per month to have access to all of the coaching group's ongoing training and positive influence. 100% of the fee can be "written off "on their taxes. If they quit this $500 now becomes income and is taxable. This will leave the doctor with maybe $250 bucks. Is it worth it?

- The most successful chiros I ever see have a coach forever, like all top performers in every field do.

- Over time a doctor begins to see their enemies with much more clarity. Not only when they try to creep into themselves, but also into others. Remember the 4 enemies are: Being lazy, weak, cheap or foolish. The high level doctor overcomes these and wins the battles against them. The lower level DC is overtaken by them, then makes excuses, or simply can't even see them.

- The Greek aphorism "Know thyself" is profound in its truth. Sometimes we all need some harsh and honest feedback to know ourselves better. We must listen and act on good feedback.

- Numbers never lie. <u>Your stats reveal what you really are and how you really think.</u> Your level of fitness and bank balance are keeping a very perfect score on your life.

- Challenge: Can you get to where you are saving more than <u>any other single bill</u> every month? Make the largest expense every month the amount you are saving. If your office rent is $3800, can you save more than this? If your mortgage is $5700 can you save more than this? This is an incredible level to reach!

Q: So It Sounds Like You Think All Chiropractors Should Become Millionaires?

Of course I do! Why did you go to school and work so hard anyway?! You did all this so you can serve people, prosper for yourself and for those you care about. It is also nice to be able to donate share, and be generous along the way. Plus it is the best thing for the profession.

One of the greatest things that could ever happen within the chiropractic profession is seeing the net worth of the entire profession grow. The more wealthy chiropractors there are the better. Money brings power and credibility like nothing else can. A profession filled with financially strong men and women is awesome.

People ask if I have a "hidden agenda" here at WINNER**SEDGE**. Of course I do. It is to <u>increase the net worth and wealth of the entire chiropractic profession</u> with what I teach, one DC at a time.

I must make it clear: It is absolutely right, just, smart, ideal, worthy, and noble to become a millionaire chiropractor. Some may want to argue with this for some unexplainable reason. That is okay. The fact will always remain that the more money you have, the more incredible things you can do for yourself and others.

People, organizations, animals, various causes out there don't need more people who care, **they need more <u>money</u>**. And if you have some, you can do some good in this world. To ever think for a second that money is evil, or whatever other line is used as an excuse by those who didn't work hard enough to have any, is an absolute joke.

Every church in this country is filled with people giving little bits of money. Yet behind the scenes there is one person who quietly walks into the church when it is totally empty, and with one signed check pays off the entire mortgage for the church. Nobody in the congregation will probably ever know. Would you rather be the "dollar bill giver" or the "thousands of dollar bills" giver?

Not only do I have Dobermans, but we also help to rescue them. What does this starved, badly abused, and recently rescued little girl need? Love? Yes, but what this little girl really needs is someone to donate some damn money to save her life. <u>Never</u> let anyone minimize the importance of becoming well-off financially. **Money can reach much farther than your hands.** There are few feelings greater than giving money where it is needed and watching the incredible good it can do!

- It is certainly a worthy goal to become a "cash millionaire."

    o A "net worth" millionaire has a net worth over a million. This occurs much sooner than the cash million usually.

    o It can occur where a doctor has just saved and saved and never paid down much debt. They could've saved $1,000,000 and still have a ton of debt. A doctor with $1,000,000 saved might actually have a negative net worth. A doctor with $50,000 saved could actually be "richer" since their net worth is greater.

- **Example 1:** A doctor has $250,000 saved but still owes $180,000 on student loans, has a first and second mortgage of $700,000 on a home worth $750,000, has credit card balances of $22,000, owes $80,000 on cars, has a boat and owes $65,000 on it, owes $30,000 on office equipment, and has past dues taxes of $28,000.

    o Add all the debt up and it is over $1,105,000 with only $250,000 saved + $50,000 in home equity. This DC has a basic Net Worth of -$605,000.

- **Example 2:** DC has $125,000 saved. Has paid all student loans, has a mortgage of $225,000 on a home worth $300,000. Only owes $8,000 on vehicles. No credit card balances or other debt.

    o Total debt = $233,000 - $200,000 in savings and equity = basic Net Worth of -$33,000.

- **Example 3:** DC has no money saved, owes $200,000 on student loans, owes $150,000 for a practice, owes $28,000 on credit cards, owes, $22,000 on a car. Basic Net Worth of -$390,000

    o This doctor is negative $390,000 but is actually $400,000 richer than the Example 1 doctor who had $250k saved!

- **Example 4:** Doctor has $750,000 saved. Owes $200,000 on a home worth $800,000. No loans, no other debt of any kind. This equals a basic Net Worth of +$1,350,000.

    o This doctor is a net worth millionaire but not a cash millionaire yet.

o Once the invested amount exceeds $1,000,000 this DC will be both a net worth millionaire and a cash millionaire. In other words, this doctor will be a REAL millionaire and is winning the game by a mile.

A common error is when a chiropractor who thinks that if they collect close to a million a year that this makes them a millionaire. I have also heard many chiropractors brag about their "million dollar practice" when in reality they have no money saved.

Should I own my building is another common question I get when it comes to space, overhead, and investing. There can be situations where a doctor should own the building they are in. There are more situations where they will for sure lose money by buying the building where they practice.

It all boils down to numbers. Just like with a home. If the principal + interest + tax + insurance + phantom payments + upkeep = significantly less than renting then consider it. I have done both.

Q: What Do You Think About Adding Associates?

I don't. What's your next question?

Q: C'mon, you must have something to say about adding associates.

Let me go over some of the main points on this ultra-simple yet ultra-complex practice scenario. There are some good associate agreements out there that are working. But...

It is so rare that adding an associate is a good idea that my answer is just NO when people have the thought of adding another doctor. This guarantees no major losses on the part of any client. I do inherit offices that already have associates. My job is to bring as much success as possible to what my client doctor might already have in place.

Consider the following points:

- Adding an associate will cost most offices at least $10,000 to well over $50,000 up front to get started. This is almost always sunk money that you will never see again.

- While you are messing with this your own practice will start to falter, <u>but you won't see it yet</u> since it is still being propelled by past momentum. The host doctor must watch his or her stats very carefully. Any drop in host doctor collections is a very real "cost" that is rarely accounted for.

- An associate must take home about $60,000 after tax in order to pay student loans and live a life similar, or a tad better than what they had as a student.

- To take home $60,000 means the associate has to earn a gross pay of $100,000.

- To earn a gross pay of $100,000 means <u>the clinic has to collect at least $200,000 more</u> to account for the <u>minimum</u> 50% overhead required to accomplish this.

- To just break even an associate must see enough people and generate enough in services to collect at least $200,000 <u>without a one dollar drop in the host doctor's collections.</u>

- This somehow must all be done in the same office space.

- It is critical to understand that two doctors require double EVERYTHING. Double the staff, double the rooms, double the chairs, double the therapy, twice as many parking spots, double the new patients, double the printing, double the phone availability, everything.

- Most of the time when there are two DCs in one office it really adds up to, in effect, 1.2 chiropractors. So why even add one?

- Very few doctors know how to plan and make a multi DC office really work. The reason is because the host DC is in an illusion. They want it to work <u>the way the want it to work</u> so badly that they can't see the **reality** of the true numbers and costs involved.

- Total collections might go up with an associate. But all the costs to do it are hidden so the host doctor makes the false conclusion that it is working. In most cases the host doctor will begin to see that their net income doesn't seem to be as much as it used to be. Bad is when the host DC tolerates this lower level.

- I can engineer these agreements in the rare event it is feasible to create a multi-doctor relationship.

- The idea of getting an associate who will do a bunch of work so you can take more time off and also take home more money is a hilarious and expensive dream in chiropractic today.

- **The dreamer DC wants the money but fails to see all that is required to have any chance of real success here.** It is a MUCH bigger project than they think or are normally capable of.

- Some dreamer doctors only have their interests in mind and have not figured out a way for the new associate to succeed. They only care about what they hope get out of the deal.

- The host doctor thinks an associate means they now get to work less but the truth is the management needs actually increase significantly. Is this not obvious? More people = more stress = more management for the host doctor.

- The host doctor wants to believe that other chiropractors are as driven as them. Very rare is the associate who has the same work ethic they do. The associate just wants to be paid to show up and see patients. It is the host DCs job to fill their book.

- A chiropractor should never be so foolish as to think anyone will care about their business as much as they do.

- The host doctor may think: *"I will just put the associate on a percentage, it's not my worry what their bills are."* Eeesh.

- It is 100% the host doctor's responsibility to create a situation where the associate can be successful.

- An associate doctor normally means more marketing. This is also expensive. The time and cost of this additional marketing alone will usually eliminate any profit the associate may bring.

- The truth is this: The associate doctor should not get paid any more than 50% of the money left after ALL expenses connected with the associate's presence are paid.

- This means that from the true <u>profit</u> generated by the associate's efforts the host doctor gets half and the associate gets half. This is fair. Under this fair deal very few associates could survive, thus proving how hard it is for this to actually work these days.

- Instead, clinic owners make an array of associate contracts each more useless than the last to try and make this work.

- The host doctor is taking all the burden and risk. All for what?

- The problem is this: It is so hard to quantify the costs in money, time, effort, stress, staff time, staff dissension, and many other things like seminar costs, buying lunches, wasted time talking to each other in the office, who pays their malpractice premium, on and on. Not to mention the endless risk exposure involved.

- Increased marketing cost, Workers Comp Insurance cost, UI cost, accounting and payroll costs, additional staff costs, cost for space, cost for supplies, stamps, equipment, etc. It all adds up to be <u>much more</u> than anyone would estimate ahead of time.

- I commonly see high volume offices compound their low collection per visit problem by adding an associate to see even more volume at their low or often no fee system. This further adds stress and a lower profit percentage for the host DC.

- The doctors here are sometimes chasing a model of: 1000 visits a week at $20 per visit = a million dollar practice. This looks easy on paper. NOT easy in real life.

- Let's say you have a male clinic owner. Another mistake is when this host doctor looks at the total collections for his two doctor office and connects this with himself as if he did it alone.

  - **Example:** A chiropractor hires an associate. They market like crazy and get to collecting $80,000 per month. The owner doctor runs around and says he has a "million dollar practice." He has a million dollar practice? But it required two DCs to do it. If there are two doctors in the office, wouldn't the new standard and goal be to have a <u>two million dollar practice</u>?

  - **Also notice here:** If you eliminated the cost of the associate, eliminated the cost of all the marketing, eliminated the cost of the extra staff, and eliminated the cost of the extra space, the chances of the host doctor having less stress and <u>more after tax take home money</u> is close to 100%. This is also much easier to sustain.

- As a chiropractor <u>you always want to connect to your own production numbers</u>. Never add anyone else's into yours or see the clinic total as a reflection of your own effort. This is a weird psychological trap which creates a false sense of achievement.

- Notice: When I say I collected $120,000 per month I will always clarify that it was <u>just me</u> and no associates because many readers will automatically think I had an associate or two.

- Yes, I did have an associate practice for about 2 years and hit $223,000 in monthly collections. The work, nuisance, and attempt at sustainability of the multi doctor office made me go back to the single doctor office of awesomeness that I now promote as the first choice for most doctors.

- I do consult many associate offices. They run about as good as possible. In every case, however, the doctor owner would take home more money, have less stress, and more time off if they went to the WINNERSEDGE single doctor, streamlined, low overhead set-up.

- I am not out to send any associate packing. But they could be converted to an Office Share or funded by the host DC to have their own office and everyone would do better in most cases.

Questions for adding an associate: If you answer "No" to any of the following questions then forget adding an associate. Please do not lie to yourself and think these do not apply to you. See the real mathematical truth and <u>seek to understand the real cost</u> of everything.

- ❏ Are you already collecting at least $700,000 per year easily?

- ❏ Do you have so many new patients that you can't handle them? (50 to 100+ new patients per month with no or little marketing.)

- ❏ Do nearly all your patients have great insurance that pays easily?

- ❏ Do you want to be married to another chiropractor and everything that comes along with their life? All the good and all the annoying, there will be both.

- ❏ Are you ready to dump <u>at least</u> $30,000 over the next 90 days to add the associate?

  - ○ How much interest would you save if this money went towards debt? Or how much interest would you lose over the years by not investing this $30,000? (These are just a few of the endless and real opportunity costs.)

- ❏ Do you have room? Will you add twice the chairs, twice the staff, twice the parking, twice the therapy, and hallways that are twice as wide? If you double the number of DCs and want to grow then you must double everything else, right?

- ❏ Are you ready and excited to work <u>more hours</u> every week to manage and market this heavier new operation?

- ❏ Are you ready and excited to hire more staff to accommodate the new doctor?

- ❏ Are you ready for the cost and pain to upgrade your software system and all billing elements to add another doctor?

- ❏ Are you ready for the mess it is to undo it all once the associate leaves? And they ALL leave sooner or later.

The doctor who thought they had to have an associate could just modify their schedule, plan their vacations and not add anyone. Over a few years they could be hundreds of thousands of dollars ahead compared to the doctor who had the "great idea" to add an associate and the infinite array of money losses that come along with it.

Sometimes a doctor who is doing incredibly well financially will want to add another doctor just for fun, or to teach the new doctor how to succeed in practice. They must accept the major cost of all this. I can make these arrangements work.

If there is a health reason and the host doctor can only work part time then an associate can be smartly engineered.

I have nothing against any doctors who associate. **I want all chiropractors to be successful.** Remember, I have many great associate DCs as clients. It is the poor planning, inadequate preparation, and the weak arrangements in the world of adding associates that I dislike.

If you are an associate and you are reading this, **REV IT UP** and be profitable where you are. Understand that you represent "overhead with two legs" and decide to <u>always generate much more than you cost.</u>

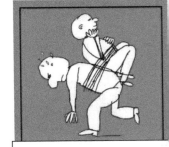

Doctors with associates almost never know how much the additional doctor really costs. They also never really know how much an associate adds to the net profit if any. In my opinion once again, if the chiropractor just stayed a single doctor office and saved every penny they would have thrown at an associate, over time they would have much more money.

Have you met my new associate? I'm going to be able to relax, take more time off, and make more money now. It's going to be great!

Multiple offices, multiple associates, partnerships, husband and wife teams, and the like are conversations for another day.

My recommendation of choice if a doctor has the room and everything required for a second doctor to flourish is to do an Office Share arrangement.

Q: Can you take a minute and tell us how an Office Share works?

This is where the second doctor is a paying tenant and not an employee. This second doctor has their own practice within the space of the existing clinic.

The new doctor has their own Tax ID, website, phone lines, software, equipment, everything. They pay rent plus their share of office expenses. They are simply renting space and sharing expenses. Here the host DC does not have any burden. With an associate the host doctor has the entire burden. I recommend the Office Share when it is viable.

WINNERSEDGE
CHIROPRACTIC CONSULTING

For DCs who want to be the most successful ever in their area.

Q: What Makes a Super Successful Chiropractor Different Than the Masses?

A more successful chiropractor or even the chiro "Super Success" thinks differently. They may even seem odd to some people. This is only because they are at a different level in many ways.

I will attempt to brain dump some of the qualities, attributes, and realizations of the super successful chiropractor.

- The super success wants to donate more to worthwhile causes.

- They are dedicated and inspiring leaders in the group, yet are still coachable and always working to get better.

- They see that making referrals and sharing is more important than sitting back saying: *"Who's gonna do something for me."*

- They avoid the amateur mistake of thinking they are "smart" or that they "know it all." In actuality, this doctor realizes how little they know, and how much they still want to learn.

- They stick with a coach forever. They don't quit at a mediocre level and say stupid things like: *"I don't need it anymore."*

- While other chiropractor's brains are turning to stone, this doctor is still playful and excited about their practice and the future.

- Money related things are not much worry. They have few bills and a surplus of money to cover them. Thoughts are redirected toward lifestyle design and reaching others.

- Practice is more exciting and fun than ever. They realize the pure joy of being a chiropractor.

- Sometimes they wonder why they didn't just feel this way all along. They know this attitude is powerful for attracting patients and good things into their lives.

- True giving emerges. Time is spent in efforts to better others and other causes. Of course this just makes even more people want to come see them in practice. They can't stop the power.

- Some think that when they have money they can cut back or quit. These doctors appreciate practice even more. Patients are automatically attracted to you more easily because of it.

- You love the fact that "chiropractic" is part of your entire identity. You respect the very profession that afforded you the opportunity to be successful and create a great life.

- You also love that you have the chiropractic lifestyle. The best lifestyle on earth. Thankfulness runs deep.

- Desire for health and fitness never loses its intensity and priority. Nobody believes how old they really are. They have clear, bright, happy eyes. They look put together and feel great versus all beat up, soft, and broken down like the masses we have dedicated our life to saving.

- This doctor sits back and thinks... *Wow am I glad I was thinking ahead on my health, my money, and my life.* They truly feel sorry for those that didn't.

- The super success recommends coaching right away. The doctor at this stage now sees the devastation that is guaranteed if a chiropractor has no organized coaching system to power them.

- They are grateful for the lessons and systems they learned years ago and say they don't know where they would be without them.

- Calls coaching the best money they ever spent by a mile. Is appreciative because they know they never would have "just made it" to this level of lifestyle on their own.

- Family, fun, vacations, and sharing is at the level they desire.

- Truly self-actualized meaning: The doctor set, worked, and reached their goals exactly or better than planned. Those who didn't are often filled with regret for past uncorrected mistakes.

- Some may say: *"Things don't always turn out as planned."* The fact is they never do for anyone. The winner has all the same things happen to them as everyone else. They just use them as fuel, learn, adapt, and grow. Many others let themselves be weakened only to then make excuses to explain their life away in an attempt to not feel so bad.

- Realization occurs that it really is pretty simple: Stay in shape, pay off debt, save systematically, see the real truth, work like hell, be able to handle the harsh criticism required to grow, see there is a God and it's not you, make no excuses, get advice from those smarter than you, and stay the course.

- The super successful doctor plans for the worst, so the worst never happens.

Q: Is It True You Call the WINNERSEDGE DC Bootcamp the Most Physically and Mentally Intense Event That Exists in Chiropractic Today?

You mean most physically and mentally intense event _ever_ in chiropractic? Yes, there is nothing like the WINNERSEDGE DC Bootcamp. It is for our members only. Nothing about it is ever discussed outside of the Bootcamp itself.

It is 32 hours of physical demolition, mental expansion, fear obliteration and mind re-conditioning. This leaves the chiropractor a better human being ready to conquer all with reckless abandon.

Nearly every doctor who does it breaks one or more major practice records within weeks after the Bootcamp. It is predicable now.

Q: Image Is Big to You, Why Does This Matter So Much in Chiropractic?

Image isn't big to me, it is big to everyone. Office image, team image, and doctor image are all critical. First impressions are everything. Recall the saying from earlier: _"What you are speaks so loud I can't hear what you're saying."_

Someone who looks like they know what they are doing will attract more people than the person who doesn't look like they know what they are doing. Perception is everything.

Chiropractors are notoriously shabby dressers. Go to any seminar and look around. I have a series of videos and entire trainings on this topic for my members. Shoes, sole thickness, socks, pants, belts, watches, shirts, cuffs, collars, ties, the correct knot, jackets, lapels, pocket scarves, jewelry, accessories, workout gear, and fit are all important. We have all this down to a science for the chiropractor.

There is no mistaking a sharp dressed man or woman. They impress or even intimidate everyone in their path and rightfully so. Effort is obvious. Effort intimidates. Effort draws respect.

Key points on Image:

- People buy with their eyes. Always remember this!
- Want to become more successful overnight? Dress better.
- *Image is ALL* - Maltz
- Who taught you how to dress anyway?
- Every socioeconomic level has its standard of dress.
- Are you letting your past control how you dress?
- You don't know how to dress successfully. Just admit it.
- The store clerks certainly don't know.
- Your boyfriend, girlfriend, hubby or wife is not the best person to ask when it comes to how to dress successfully for work.
- What to wear is scientifically determined and has been for years. Follow this information or there is a price to pay in lost income.
- *Every girl's crazy 'bout a sharp dressed man.* -ZZ Top
- *Every woman loves a man in* _____. It's true.
- What is the official chiropractic uniform?
- Every professional man and woman should have at least one perfect fitting suit from top to bottom.
- You should dress <u>better</u> than your best dressed patients.
- When you dress well, you feel better. This attracts people.
- Shoes are key. A chiropractor must <u>always</u> wear good shoes.

     I could spend a lot of time on this, but that is not the focus of this book. Suffice to say that wearing the right uniform to work will make more people listen to you <u>and</u> follow you. ***How you dress controls how other people treat you.*** Image plus personality are unstoppable. You must dress well as a chiropractor.

What is wrong with the picture on the right? What seems odd? What is out of place? Who is the gray haired guy?

It is success legend Bob Proctor. Every chiro should know Proctor's work well. I met him at a high-level seminar I attended with him and his team. It cost $18,300 for a three-day seminar and over $20,000 when it was all said and done.

On the evening before the seminar there was a casual meet and greet in the hotel lobby. After some mingling I walked up to him and as I was about to shake his hand he quickly looked me up and down with his eyes as if to say: *"What the ____ are you wearing?"*

I will never forget this! Why did he do this?

He is at a higher socioeconomic level than I am. It was his event and I failed to acknowledge and respect him by dressing properly. (There were over 100 people attending from all over the world. I estimate he profited easily over $2,400,000 in <u>one weekend</u>.)

I should have been wearing a perfect suit! Now, the broke and clueless might say: *"It shouldn't matter what you wear, he should judge you for who you are!"* (That is why they are broke and certainly clueless. Image matters so much it is beyond important.)

No one cares who you are unless you first LOOK like someone they want to know in the first place.

Those who know how people and society really operate know that this was an embarrassing situation for me. I screwed up royally. I could never take back this weak first impression.

I knew the second he looked me up and down that I was lazy and foolish by not bringing and wearing a perfect suit, like <u>he had done for me and all his other guests.</u> I disrespected him and everyone there. I knew it and he knew it.

My "million dollar practice" meant <u>nothing</u> to him. I was not so special that I could say: *"I'm paying for this so I will wear whatever I want.*" That is what losers say. And he thought of me as a loser even though I was already quite successful. I am still upset about this. He is a true legend in the world of increasing human potential.

Either way, I was certified as a Bob Proctor Life Success Consultant. It is pretty cool to be licensed to teach his material.

Now at my own seminars I will wear a perfect suit and be amazed at the doctors who do not understand that <u>if they just looked better, more people would for sure come to them.</u>

Dress better and you will automatically become more successful. It is mysteriously powerful. The tragedy is, the doctor heads to the mall and has no idea what to buy or where to buy it. They remain lost and dull as far as their wardrobe and image go.

The backwards chiropractor can errantly think: *"I will dress better after I am collecting more."* Wrong! You must look better <u>first,</u> then you will collect more. Just buy one nice clothing item at a time.

Watch this: The picture above was a random shot on a break at one of my seminars. Now you tell me who collects the most? In fact, can you put them in order of collections from the highest collecting doctor to the lowest in the group at the time this picture was taken? You'd be right. Notice how image and money mysteriously and automatically go together. Fascinating isn't it?

When you talk about money, image will ALWAYS enter into the conversation. They are connected. The key question here is: Do the more successful chiropractors dress better after they are successful, or before?

Q: This May Be an Odd Question. How Many Years of Experience Do You Think Your Consulting Adds To the 20 Years You've Already Been Practicing?

Hmm. How many years would you have to practice to draw 100 office floorplans, oversee the hiring of hundreds of CAs, plus the thousands of marketing, office system, and money questions?

Maybe 1000 years. I don't know. The goal is to be valuable and use what I have learned. Information does no good if it just sits in someone's head. This is why I have an instant video library with over 500 videos for my clients. It is growing all the time.

I take what I learn and get it into video form so others can use it. This makes us very unique.

Q: Should Chiropractors Go to An All Cash Practice?

Few chiropractors should do that just yet. We have Medicare patients, personal injury patients, work injury patients, insurance patients, and cash patients. My official teaching is to become an expert at ALL of these in your state.

It would take a very powerful and persuasive chiropractor to take all past and incoming patients and throw them into the cash bucket.

A new doctor, in their own hometown, who knows everyone, and can get 100 new patients their first month, plus has a simple office with super low overhead could do it with good coaching.

I can teach an existing or new chiropractor how to go cash. It takes a significant amount of philosophy, dedication, and work.

It also depends on the state a chiropractor is in. In some states insurance is still fairly easy. In other states there is basically no insurance. The doctors in these states are more cash based to begin with.

Here at WINNERSEDGE we can coach every type of office from all PI, heavy insurance, to all cash. We are also prepared for the full-on cash practice future that inevitably awaits our profession. For most states though, I recommend a chiropractor be an expert and still accept some insurance. Maximize it and pay down debt. The key is to pay down debt.

We are heading into an era where there is huge school debt and no insurance. So the doctor has no choice but to become a very good chiropractor and a great marketer. <u>When people actually have to pay for care themselves you better be good</u>. When insurance is paying most of the bill, many patients will go just to use their benefits.

It is a major awakening when a doctor has a cranking practice where many local companies offer the same great insurance. This chiro has a ton of insurance patients and entire families coming in all the time.

Then overnight the insurance plans change. They go to $4500 deductibles or the doctor is kicked out of the network because Acme Ins. Co. thought they were paying the doctor too much. The patients now have to pay. Many disappear. What a letdown it is when the chiropractor sees that patients were only coming in because it was cheap and not because they were so great.

Want to know how good you are as a chiropractor? Two stats tell the story. Which ones are they? **Patient Referrals and Patient Visit Average.** How many referrals are you getting + how long do people stay with you = how good you are. Notice nowhere in here is your collections. Referrals and PVA are chiropractic skill measures. Collections are more a location, marketing, and business skill measure.

I have already designed three different versions of the ultra-low overhead chiropractic office of the future. I have them ready to roll out if and when the time comes. We fear nothing here. There is a saying when it comes to insurance: *"It is getting so bad that it is actually getting good."* Once everyone knows that insurance will not pay, it will be even easier to start people under care. The trick is when they "think" they are covered, and you have to tell them that they are not.

Q: What Are the Best States to Practice In?

The state you want to live in is always the best state to practice in. <u>You bring success to wherever you are.</u> To give you an idea: It takes 300 visits a week in Wisconsin to collect what 120 visits a week will collect in Illinois, Pennsylvania or New Jersey. It is amazing to see the differences on all the stat sheets I get every month. I see DCs collecting $117 per visit down to doctors at $15 per visit.

Mostly cash plus little insurance in an area with a high cost of living, compared to practicing in an area where insurance still gives money away and you can pay a CA $12 per hour and buy a sweet 6000 sq. ft. home on one acre with a pool for $500,000.

In South Dakota you cannot have a patient pay for even one visit in advance. They are not allowed to pay for anything until <u>after</u> the service has been rendered, let alone prepay for 50 visits. In Florida if a patient's neck itches, some Lawyers will have them in for a surgical consult without even telling you.

A variety of scenarios are out there. Go where you want to live or where you want to end up living. Waste no time anywhere but where you really want to be. Moving is costly.

	Total	Goal
PVA	26	30
Case Avg.	2981	3500
Svc's/Vis	191	192
Coll/Vis	114	120
% Coll.	40	60

	Total	Goal
PVA	52	29
Case Avg.	1125	1,333
Svc's/Vis	76	80
Coll/Vis	85	46
% Coll.	96	58
Automatics		

	Total	Goal
Visits	443	360
PI Vis	17	13
New Pt's	17	34
New PI/PR	3/27	21
Resigns	16	9
Services	84565	83600
Tot Collect.	50676	46000
PI Collect	2550	2000
Ins Collect	38785	30400
Pt Coll.	11939	9000
Massages	235	132
Mass. Coll.	11290	6336

	Total	Goal
Visits	709	800+
New Pt's	19	30+
New PI	5	5+
Referrals	18	20+
Resigns	8	17+
Services	53551	20,000+
Ins Collect	1521	5000+
Pat Collect	6353	20,000+
PI Collect	6285	15,000+
Total Coll	24749	40,000+

The doctor on the left doesn't work all that hard, shows up, sees 443 visits a month and collects $50,676. The DC on the right is working his tail off, sees 709 visits and collects $24,749. Look at the Insurance collections. A major state to state difference.

Q: What Do You Feel Are the Biggest Problems Facing Chiropractors Today and In the Future?

There are no real problems outside the chiropractor's own mind. The world is fine. Chiropractic is fine. Almost everyone has an issue they would see a chiropractor for. Chiropractic is affordable. Chiropractic is convenient. The public's aversion to medicine is pushing people towards more natural approaches. Chiropractic is the undisputed champion in this arena. <u>We are positioned perfectly for the future!</u>

There are already chiropractors doing well everywhere as proof. There are coaches like me that can literally spoon feed everything a DC needs to know one video at a time. Unlike when I started, there were no such things as websites, online coaching videos, bootcamps, cheap color printing, every door direct mail, smartphones, YouTube or Google.

It is actually so easy to build a practice today that the only element required is a chiropractor with a work ethic to do it.

It's just a matter of whether or not a man or woman chiropractor can build themselves into the three required people: The **Promoter** of chiropractic, the **Chiropractor,** and the smart **Businessperson.** <u>A doctor must become great in all three of these required categories.</u>

To answer your question, here are several things I see that hold chiropractors back. I am going to be harsh:

1. **Inability to work hard for sustained periods of time**. The new doctor works a little for a few minutes, needs to be praised for being a good little doctor, then needs a break to go play.

    - I started working 7am to 7pm Monday thru Friday and Sat am. Starting a practice is a 100 hour per week deal.

2. **No effort to learn the philosophy** of chiropractic despite observing that practically <u>all</u> the most successful chiros on earth have HUGE philosophy. I talk to chiros who cannot understand why a person would need more than a few adjustments. Huh?

    - Truth is: <u>Every human being on earth could get adjusted at the end of every day of their life</u> to keep as many Foruns flowing as possible. If you don't know what a "Forun" is you are way behind in your philosophy.

3. **Inability to figure things out.**

    - A doctor asks me for another DC's name. He wants to ask the guy a question about something he heard him say at a recent seminar. I email the name. The doctor then emails me back saying: *"Do you also have the guy's phone number?"* My first thought is: *"I just gave you the name, why didn't you just Google him?"*

4. **Inability to start and finish the projects needed to grow.**

   - I tell a doctor to put a short video of themselves on their website. They reply back: *"What do I say?"* or *"How do I do that,"* even though they have mine to copy word for word and a device in their hand, or at their desk that has ALL THE WORLD'S INFORMATION ON HOW TO DO EVERYTHNG AVAILABLE IN SECONDS.

5. **Sheer weakness.** It takes a certain drive to own a business, be an entrepreneur, and grow a practice. Society and school today tend to breed soft, easily hurt, weak, sissified crybabies who can't take the pain and grind of real physical and mental work.

   - This relates to an inability to sacrifice <u>now</u> for more success <u>later</u>. Inability to delay gratification. They want to feed their senses now at the expense of much bigger success later. They do "wants" before "needs."

6. **Arrogance and lack of accountability.** Doctors who shake a hand or sign their name, but when it comes down to it, don't want to be held responsible for what they just agreed to.

   - A new doctor joins a coaching group under a special 24 month *New DC Start Up* program. The coach designs the office, provides all the systems, scripts, business set-up, procedures, key marketing materials, marketing plan, and CA training. Everything is perfect. Not in a hundred years, even with any other group could this DC have been set up any better. The doctor gets going a couple months then suddenly sends an email and wants to quit the program. There is a simple and fair termination fee in the rare event that a weak and foolish decision like this might occur. This doctor calls the coach a "bully" for trying to get them to pay the early termination fee even though the doctor <u>already agreed and signed their name to it when they joined</u>.

   - This is an example of no honor. This doctor's handshake and signature mean <u>nothing</u>. This *"I want to do whatever I want with no consequence"* type of thinking is a disgrace to themselves, their family, and chiropractic.

- Life and practice deliver severe and expensive lessons to people like this.

7. **Technical incompetence.** The inability to find and actually adjust vertebra. When I started, my only concern was whether or not I could find and adjust subluxations successfully. I wanted to be great at <u>chiropractic</u>. I wanted to get people better. I wanted to help the hard cases. I wanted to be one of the few chiropractors getting the results that make chiropractic famous. I wanted to be good at the really difficult to perform adjustments that very few in the profession can do.

   - Today the "chiropractic" is almost incidental in many chiropractic offices. It is as though the newer doctor just assumes they are good and has no idea how much of a "hack" they really are.

   - The great chiropractors in history are great and revered to this day because they were **great chiropractors**. A lost art. It's not lost with me though.

   - You cannot talk about money in chiropractic without technique entering the conversation. Money is a result of our results. Our results come from the application of our technique.

8. **Poor money handling.** The doctor thinks all the money they collect is theirs when in reality only a small part of it really is.

9. **Lack of coaching.** Doctors who think they can do well without the massive help from a coach are foolish. There is too much to know. There are too many landmines and traps to avoid.

   - Why waste all the time, pain, and cost to get experience when you can <u>just buy it and use it right now</u> via a consultant. It is the fastest and most efficient way.

10. **Sheer desire and drive.** The will to win. The work ethic. The *charge* to do something impressive. The motivation to wake up and want to build your brand. The energy to go after something, to defend something, to create something! The ability to get PUMPED UP and want to rock and roll. <u>The might to get the work done</u> that matters for something.

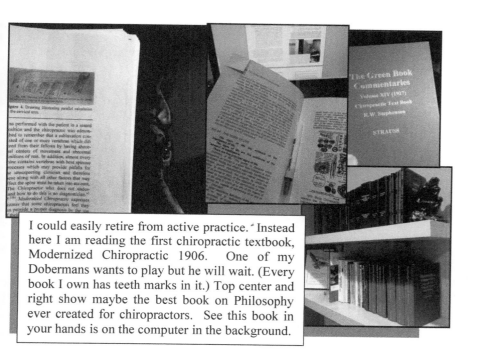

I could easily retire from active practice. ˙ Instead here I am reading the first chiropractic textbook, Modernized Chiropractic 1906.   One of my Dobermans wants to play but he will wait. (Every book I own has teeth marks in it.) Top center and right show maybe the best book on Philosophy ever created for chiropractors. See this book in your hands is on the computer in the background.

Q: What Do All the Most Successful Chiropractors You Know Have in Common?

This is a great question. Warren Buffet says: *"When it comes to evaluating people I look for three things:"*

1. **Integrity** (Integrity = Honor!)

2. **Intelligence**

3. **Energy**

The big winners in chiropractic possess all three of these. The goal is to be a person of **integrity**, who has and uses their **intelligence**, and has the **energy** to make things happen. All the powerhouses I know have these three. A few other qualities that come to mind are:

1.   They listen to those who know more than they do.

2.   They work hard ON their practice as well as IN it.

3.   They get things done NOW.

4. They have an unbelievable belief and conviction for chiropractic. They are philosophy giants.

5. They pay the price to get really good at everything.

6. They know money will follow their great service.

7. They look successful, even if wearing jeans and a t-shirt.

8. Their office, home, and cars are always sharp and clean.

9. They understand: *"How you do anything is how you do everything."*

10. They obviously have their money system in order like a thing of beauty.

11. They are patient with people, but don't waste time.

12. They know and are directed by this truth: *"The needs of the many outweigh the wants of the few."*

13. They have the correct treatment time vs. are *"still working on it."* They had a slow treatment time. Key word is had. They now have a correct treatment time.

14. They do what is not convenient. They make sacrifices knowing that the return is greater than whatever they thought they would be missing.

15. The best athletes on earth train when they "don't feel like it." Similarly, the successful doctor goes to trainings and seminars when they "don't feel like it."

16. They understand that coaching does not cost money. It is simply a trade. A trade of their small amount of money to get a larger amount in return. The super successful DC makes good money trades all the time. The poor DC fails to make the trades, or makes trades that return nothing, or actually lose money.

17. They are highly conditioned physical specimens. The most successful doctors I have ever known get up between 4:30 and 6 at the latest. They work out nearly every day and get more done in a day than some do in a week.

18. They are happy, cool, and very nice, yet don't take sh*t from anyone. Like Clint Eastwood for example: Always nice, quiet, cool, skilled, and smart, but if you cross them, break their trust, have no honor, lie, or mess with them, you are going to pay. It is our Doberman Philosophy in action.

19. They will stay as late as it takes. Go in as early as it takes. Pay whatever it takes. Study whatever is needed. Attend whatever events are required. Eliminate whatever needs to be eliminated. Add whatever needs to be added. Learn whatever needs to be learned, and then apply it all in order to grow and reach more people in a positive way.

20. They plan time off and have a lot of fun. They play hard.

21. They read, and then read more.

22. They seem to walk more powerfully than everyone else.

23. When they talk you know they are telling the truth.

24. They explain things very well, even when explaining complex things to a child.

25. They are on time. They will be there when they say they will. Reminding them is never necessary.

26. If you need to hear the truth they will dish it clear and sharp.

27. They tip well. They tip in advance when it is smart to do so. They tip more when they know it might make a difference in the person's day.

28. They leave money lying around anonymously. They plant money seeds that will return a harvest.

29. They donate money religiously and would like to give more.

30. They are respectful to animals and all God's creatures. Some may be hunters of course, but are respectful and in awe of nature and its awesomeness.

31. Of course all bills are paid on time or in advance.

32. They are the kind of people that others love to do business with, so they usually get better service and more for their money everywhere they go.

33. They call the patients who need a call. They meet after hours patients when needed. They care more. This is another reason why their patients love and refer to them.

34. They have a Plan B, Plan C and Plan D for their tough patients. They do not care who gets the credit as long as the person gets better.

35. They can refer a patient to another chiropractor without their ego being hurt.

36. They figure out how to do things they don't already know how to do. They hate to hide behind the words. *"I don't know how to do that."* They figure out how to do it, and quickly if needed.

37. They are happy and smile a lot in contrast to those walking around anxious, nervous, uptight, or whiny all the time.

38. They are prepared and rarely caught off guard.

39. They tell stories well. And everyone listens when they do.

40. They do not care about being popular. If it happens that is fine, but they don't seek it.

41. They are the one who everyone looks to when it all hits the fan. They will know what to do.

42. You can see in their eyes that they have it together. You can see the confidence and coolness. No sorrow or regret is hiding back there. It has already been dealt with.

43. They never shine the trophy or feel they have arrived.

44. They are great planners for the future, for themselves, and for those they care about.

45. They live the chiropractic power life. Chiropractic, nutrition, drugless, healthy, natural whenever possible. Their life proves they believe and trust in innate intelligence.

46. They share advice when asked. They like to see others do well. They know that to continue to succeed they must bring increase to others.

47. Everyone loves to be adjusted by them because they know they are good. They have put in massive effort to be that way. Plus you know that they know they are good. You want to be on the receiving end of it.

48. They are not a chiropractor. They are the human representation of chiropractic itself. They are chiropractic.

49. They have "won't power" as well as will power. They have the power to say NO and mean it.

50. They are deeply grateful and know that health, life and time are precious. They can all be gone in a flash.

51. Most I know care about their eternal future. They can see through all the massive lies and corruption on earth. They know there is a God. They understand God's fairness. They know that no matter how good they are, they have still broken God's laws. For that a penalty must be paid. They know that either they will have to pay for it, or that Jesus's sacrificial death is sufficient to pay for it if they believe, trust, and accept this gift of God's grace. Which they do. God is fair and just: If one rejects God here, He rejects them when they die. If one believes God while here, He rewards them when they die. It is fair. The DC never assumes their finite mind can question the infinite Creator of the universe.

Basically, the super successful DC **is the real thing themselves.**
Key truth: *The law of emulation states that the more you behave like a super successful chiropractor, the more you will then become one yourself.*

Every video, every CD, every event, every email, every call, every piece of written material, everything we do here at WINNERSEDGE is designed with the intention of transforming and developing chiropractors into this person.

Our **Bootcamp Extreme** is the perfect example. Change requires intensity. This event provides the intensity and immersion that is required to cause real, immediate, and permanent change.

Q: What Are Your Recommendations as Far as Working Out, Nutrition, and Other Ways For Chiropractors To Keep Their Energy High?

I will just give you some bullets or else we will be here all day for this question. I have some very strong opinions on this topic. Many people do.

Here's what I do:

- I make my own cereal based on granola, raw almonds, sunflower nuts, Goji berries, wheat germ, etc. I pour about one inch in a bowl with unsweetened Coconut milk or Hemp milk. It is very clean, fast, and I look forward to it every day.

- I train, primarily with bodyweight and Kettlebells every workday morning at 7 am. I go 30 minutes hard. I have a trainer who is one of the top Kettlebell trainers in the US. I am also RKC certified and trained by Pavel himself. (Those who know, will know what this means.)

- I drink filtered and fluoride free water during the day and have nothing to eat until my lunch at 2:00. I will have gone about 8 hours with no food. My stomach never growls and my energy never falters. I am running on dinner the night before. Breakfast and lunch are just small carryover meals to me.

Pavel Tsatsouline above: The force behind the Russian Kettlebell revolution in America. He is an incredibly impressive person and is a LOT stronger than he looks. Me and my Trainer Kurt Hartmann. He also is a lot stronger than he looks. It is important to have great training influences in your life.

- Lunch is simple. One organic bar of a few different varieties I like with a glass of organic coconut water. Sometimes a piece of fruit too, but I find that fruit makes me tired. I eat lunch at my desk, it takes about 5 min and I roll on. My day is 11 hours straight. I like to get about 10 to 10.5 hours of legit work done.

- After lunch it is more filtered water. Dinner at about 8. I make a big salad. I stand and chop organic radishes, carrots, celery, green onions, olives, kidney beans, broccoli, lettuce, and spinach. I use Olive Oil and Balsamic Vinegar for dressing.

- Dinner consistently varies from salmon, to chicken, to no meat, or even just a heavy green drink of kale, ginger, carrots, apples, celery, cucumbers, and spinach. Popeye had it right along!

- My goal is to always have all micronutrients, phytonutrients and minerals present in my system so I can be as smart as possible. Plus for energy and working out.

- Mental work also burns a lot of fuel so complete nutrition is key. Lots of raw food of a variety of different colors is what I'm after.

- Key: Dinner is when you fill the tank for the next day. Breakfast and lunch are just place holder meals to tide me over until dinner.

- The typical American eats 500 calories too many every day. Mostly from breakfast, snacks, and lunch.

- My results speak for themselves. My ideal weight for my height is 184 and right this second I am at 184.8 with clothes on and feel great 99.99% of the time.

- I do not care what any person on earth says about nutrition if they are not personally at their ideal weight and/or in serious physical condition.

- If a person is overweight, then their body is already carrying a lot of stored fuel, so no lunch is required. Most people eat because of habit vs. out of necessity.

- Eating between meals makes no sense to me or sense biologically. We have a stomach and digestive system designed to take and process one pile of food in one sequence. Sending it bits and pieces all day long makes no sense. And it certainly makes no sense for digestion and elimination.

- Studies have shown that blood sugar does not rise and fall if you miss meals. Your body has plenty of fat to burn to keep your blood sugar on par. It is just cravings people feel.

- Basic idea: Eat morning fuel → Drink water → Eat midday fuel → Drink water → Eat Evening fuel to fill tank → Water with fruit chopped in it for after dinner snack.

- Now I am not bodybuilding, preparing for a fight or for an Ironman. I am talking about day to day chiropractor stuff here. Obviously specific sports will have their fueling needs.

- If looking to lean-up some, you can make modifications like only having a glass of coconut water for lunch.

- If I had a big dinner on Friday night, the next morning I might only have a big glass of the water I get from a local spring with a lemon in it. That's all I will have until about 2:00.

- Without a doubt, I find I'm at my absolute smartest, sharpest, most creative, and most clear when there is nothing anywhere in my system. Observe: Last night I fueled my body fully. It was all absorbed overnight and is now ready to be used. The next morning I have my water, it triggers the gastro enteric reflex so I eliminate. My system is clear, I'm hydrated and now in perfect form to get mental work done. It works.

- People eat too much and too often. It is a lack of discipline. It is weakness. It is a lack of "won't power."

- Of course I love to eat, but as I see it, you fuel according to the need. If you have eaten a ton and not burned it, then back off. You should easily be able to fast for 12 to 24 hours. It is good for your system to have a break.

- I am in preservation mode. I want to go years, even decades and look the same. I tell everyone I am 28. There is a powerful psychological trick I am invoking by doing this.

- Elimination is key. Eat then eliminate. Everyone is hung up on what to shove in their face. Elimination of waste via sweating and digestion is just as critical.

- Sure, I will have a few pizzas in a year, but the overwhelming majority of my fueling is on point. In fact, if I have pizza, I will follow it with apples in water or some green drink so I don't feel so bad for sending trash through my system.

- I will not be like the masses of weak and sick people everywhere. People are counting on me to be sharp and in shape. I take this responsibility seriously. When a patient walks in, or I deal with a chiropractor client, <u>I want them to get my physical and mental best at all times.</u>

- A favorite dessert of mine: Organic apples chopped up in my killer spring water. *An apple a day keeps the_____.* What if it is true? Also great for elimination. Blackberries or chopped strawberries in water are also great. Teach kids this.

- I basically never drink. Sure, I've partied some in the past but my priorities are different now. I will, however, after each of the 5 seminars I teach have one stiff shot of Jack Daniels or a Vodka James Bond Martini.

- I do this just to remind myself how much I hate alcohol. And to burn my throat. It burns like hell. I do this to humble myself just in case I was starting to think I was special after being on a stage all day. It may seem weird, but that's what I do.

After a Bootcamp once I brought everyone back to my house. They were physically and mentally beat. Some were saying: *"Oh great, I'd really like a cold beer."* Nope, you will get Vita Mix monster smoothies and power juices and like it!

Getting into a rhythm is the key. The body loves consistency. Eat and eliminate. Train this.

I have never had a cup of coffee in my life. Caffeine is a drug, sugar is a drug, alcohol is a drug. Any one of them can start to control you. And sadly do for many people.

I am very proud that I never let any such thing start to control me. I never *"have to have my coffee"* or *"need a drink after work"* or any other such *"I let myself get addicted because I was weak"* habits.

People love to make excuses for this stuff. They are all hilarious. Body fueling is ridiculously simple. Eat God-made food when you need it, drink good water, eliminate well, work out hard, done.

Eat food that was made by the Sun. The Sun gives energy to the plants. You then eat the plants, which means you get all that energy. If you eat what is dead what do you think you get?

Supplements, some are real and decent. Most are garbage and everyone knows it, but they lie and talk about how great they are if they can make a buck. I sell none. Selling supplements in a chiro office is for DCs who are bad at math. Question: *What do supplements have anything to do with chiropractic?* Answer: *Nothing.*

The Triune of LIFE is Intelligence, Force, and Matter. Chiropractic is only concerned with the Force part. Supplements, medicine, even working out are trying to change the matter. Not that this is bad. It is just not chiropractic.

I love good supplements, pillows, mattresses, braces, ice packs, orthotics, and all these things. I coach DCs who sell everything. It is just hard to actually make a penny doing it when the doctor could be delivering adjustments, making a much greater impact with people and for much more profit.

If you take 7 minutes to talk to a patient about supplements, you could have adjusted 5 people and collected say instead.

Chiropractic is so powerful and efficient that almost anything a DC could do otherwise will certainly lose money. Many never see or find out the hard way how true this really is.

You might call them: **Phantom money losses.** These are all the never seen money losses that a chiropractor creates for themselves by wasting time on less important and less profitable activities.

Adding a person to "do the nutrition for you" is a great and noble idea. In virtually all cases this ends up being just another elaborate way that chiropractors find to take home even less money.

On top of something that makes little money to begin with, they go and add the most expensive thing possible, another person. This only bogs the doctor down even further with managerial and marketing responsibility to keep this person going. People like this and massage therapists normally can never get any new people for themselves.

I once consulted a chiropractic office that was collecting over $9000 a month for nutrition. They had never really analyzed the cost to do this. After closer analysis it was revealed that they spent $7000 on the products and still had to pay the nutrition practitioner they hired. All said and done they were losing about $500 per month even though nutrition "looked" like it was collecting $9000. Remember, the most successful DCs are the best at the real math and costs in their practice.

Know the opportunity cost for time. At $30+ per minute what could you possibly do that is more valuable than adjusting spines?

At around $1000 per hour or more, why would a chiropractor do anything other than try to adjust as many people as they could? Doing so in as simple an office as possible, with the lowest overhead possible?

The creative, well-meaning ways that chiropractors find to give away their profit are endless. We can save that for another booklet.

Q: Is It True That the Top 10% Of Chiropractors Are Taking Home 90% Of All the Money That Is Being Collected In Chiropractic Today?

Yeah that's about right. Amazing isn't it? This is true in almost all industries. Look at what the CEO of US Bank earns. Let's say it is $12,000,000 a year. How many lower level employee salaries does it take to add up to the CEOs? It takes 300 employees earning $40,000 a year to add up to just his salary alone.

The key point here is that he totally deserves it. The weak thinking underachiever might say: "*Nobody deserves to be paid that much money.*" Oh yes they do! If you could run a huge corporation like that they would happily give you the money. I am quite certain you would happily take it. So would I!

It is amazing how many people will make fun of others who are doing well. What does this mean? Why do people do this? If it were you or I doing well financially we wouldn't like people making fun of us, or telling us we didn't deserve it would we?

Additional points:

- Be happy when others are successful. <u>Appreciate success wherever you see it</u>. This is a very important attitude to have.

- Be happy for others if they excel you. You would want them to do the same for you right?

- Great quote from Samuel "Golden Rule" Jones: "*What I want for myself, I want for everyone!*"

- Give! Top people in all fields are great referrers. They look to GIVE referrals whenever possible. They know this is what sparks a huge return.

- The lower level thinker only wants to <u>get</u> referrals. Again it is the "me" attitude versus the "them" attitude. The "them" mindset always wins.

- The winners want results and don't care about recognition. Why would they want recognition, they just did what they were supposed to be doing anyway.

- When CAs do something well, don't overpraise. Acknowledge with a kind word and a smile of course. Great and dedicated work is what they are <u>supposed to do anyway</u>. No need for celebrating unless they did something great or hit a new *Best*.

- People ask about family balance. In my life everyone knows that I am on a mission. Either they are with it or they are not in my life. Quote: "*When she married me, she knew she was marrying the mission too.*"

- Family must understand that the extra work which must be done brings a reward and a lifestyle they then enjoy. There is nothing worse than hearing: *"Honey why do you have to go to the office today"* as they drive their BMW to see their personal trainer, stop by LuLu Lemon for some shopping, then back home to lay by the pool in the backyard.

- It is okay for you to say: *"Hey, where do you think all this stuff comes from?"* Be nice of course.

- The top chiropractors are on top of things. They have their stats to me first at the end of the month. They watch all new videos first. They "go first" when such situations arise. In the fight world there is a common saying: *"Be first!"*

Q: What Is a Good Way to Determine What You Can Or Can't Really Afford?

There are many ways. This question is very simple to answer. All of us are so used to operating our financial lives differently that it can be confusing. I will use an example that will put things in perspective.

Imagine you just sold your car. It is gone. You have no car. It is now time for you to get a different car. There are only two rules you have to follow as you start looking at vehicles. **Rule #1** is: You can only buy what you can pay cash for. No financing, no credit cards, no borrowing of any kind is allowed. You must write a check for your next car. **Rule #2**: You must buy it by the end of the day tomorrow.

Question: What could you truly afford?

Really think about this. How much cash do you have right now available to buy a car with? This is what you can really afford. This will be shocking to people.

Would it be a $4000 Honda with high miles? Would it be a $15,000 truck? Could it be a $164,000 Maserati? Many could only afford a $2000 pile, and some might not be able to get any car at all.

Do you realize there was a time when it used to be this way? People used to just write a check for their car. Most households only had one vehicle. Then financing emerged. Auto and truck prices zoomed up and here we are today with cars that cost more than most people earn in a year of work. Isn't that crazy?

Imagine if right now everyone on the road instantly had the car they were driving switched for the car they could truly afford with no help from anyone or any bank. Wouldn't that be interesting?

The answer to the question is: For <u>everything</u> other than education and a house, if you cannot pay cash, you really can't afford it.

Imagine how rich you could be if you actually lived like this.

There was a time it was embarrassing to even let anyone see you with a Credit Card because it meant you didn't have the money to pay. In the current era most people who use them still don't have the money to pay, it's just now the embarrassment factor has been intentionally and systematically erased from society.

Now everyone thinks that if they can swing the monthly payments this means that they can afford it. Good for banks, bad for us.

I had another interesting idea: Just for fun lets have all men and women going out to socialize wear a t-shirt that has their credit score <u>and</u> total money they have saved printed in **BIG NUMBERS** on the front of it. Wouldn't this change the dynamics of the social scene?

Q: Do You Have Any Advice for The Chiropractor Who Wants to Treat More Athletes?

A lot of new chiropractors say this and it somewhat concerns me. It can be a limiting thought. A 40-year-old woman with headaches is as important as any NFL football player. As far as I'm concerned, no people need chiropractic more than anyone else. Everyone needs it badly. I want EVERYONE coming in to see me.

I hear newer chiropractors ask me: *"How can I get in to work on athletes?"* or *"How do I get in to work on <u>Pro</u> Athletes?"* This usually means I am talking to a doctor who wants to "say" they treat big athletes before they have actually become any good as a chiropractor.

This doctor may want the applause before they have actually learned how to perform. It is like saying you want to drive a 300 mile per hour dragster a month after you received your driver's license. You have to work up to these things.

Treating high level athletes is not the type of thing you want to start with. The same goes for the Personal Injury practice. I have operated an almost all cash practice and done well. When I moved to Minneapolis and reached 100+ visits a day I again had quite a few PI patients. I was forced to get good at PI. At one point I averaged over 100 PI visits every week alone.

It all starts by building a big practice. Once you have done this and gain the experience, you can go after certain types of patients more. Early on though, you want everyone to come and see you. I believe I heard Sid Williams once say: *"Get to 500 visits a week then learn how to make money."* There is some truth to this. There are also some problems with this. Once you start letting everyone come in for cheap, or let all kids come in for free, it is almost impossible to correct it.

If a chiropractor wants to treat more athletes and even Olympic and Pro athletes do this:

1. Become really good at examining spines by hand.

2. Become really good at adjusting spines and extremities by hand.

3. Build a practice that sees at least 50 patients a day. 100 or more patients a day is much better yet. The 100 a day chiropractor will have <u>double</u> the experience compared to the 50 a day DC. (Often double the PI, and athletes, and everything.)

4. Go to events where you can meet people doing the activities you want to be involved with.

5. Find a way to sponsor them. <u>Be a booster, sponsor, or something</u>. You can pay to have a banner in a local gym all the way up to sponsoring an Olympian.

6. Understand there is usually more grind than glory in this.

At one point early on in practice we had the head football coach of the local high school, assistant head coach, head basketball coach, assistant basketball coach, state champion golfer, star women's basketball player, quarterback of the football team, a few star basketball players, their parents, soccer players, the Principal of the school, and

Vice Principal plus more as patients. At the time I didn't think anything of it. Looking back I realize how incredible this really was.

Do well at taking care of high school athletes. Then all of a sudden you get a college kid or two. If you deliver the goods then you get more. Then if someone becomes pro at something then you've got them. It just happens if you are good and can fix things. People go to the chiropractor who can find and adjust subluxations the best.

Results bring people. ALWAYS remember that! It all hangs on results. **If you work to get results and not athletes, then you will have as many athletes as you want coming to you for results.**

Many doctors want the higher profile patients before they can actually fix anything or are even capable of handling such people. How you care for a College, Olympic, or Pro athletes of any kind is a whole different game of risk. You have got to be very perceptive and aware.

Experience is key. If a doctor wants to see more athletes, or PI for that matter, then the solution is to get good and see a lot of people. Reach 100+ patients a day and you will have a lot of everything, trust me on this.

Another point to make here is that if you really want "in" the higher levels YOU MUST BE WILLING TO PAY. Sure, you can see some athletes through the normal course of practicing and socializing. But if you want to be serious then you must be willing to pay. If you see my clinic name on a Banner, or top ranked fighters shorts Live on FOX in front of 10 million people how do you think it got there?

I never pursued athletes and recommend you don't either. Just get good at helping everyone you can and allow it to happen. Athletes are normally crummy patients who never make their visits, want it for free, have parents you have to deal with, coaches to worry about, trainers and team physicians opposing you, and many other considerations and risky scenarios that make this world a lot different than you think.

Let me say I recommend the Gonstead Seminars personally if you want to get better as a chiropractor. I am not aware of any Seminar in chiropractic that teaches chiropractors how to examine and adjust spines more thoroughly. The CCSP is also an incredible credential.

Dr. Tory wrestling with Big Ten Champ, Kevin Wilmot!

To Tory,
Thanks for
the adjustment!
from the silent warrior,
Cael Sanderson

CAEL SANDERSON
159-0

My favorite sport is fighting. Like UFC. It is a sport that perfectly parallels chiropractic. I have cared for countless fighters, teams, trainers, from entry level to champions. As I write this I am preparing to leave for International Fight Week in Las Vegas. It all started because 19 years ago I made <u>really good adjustments on one guy</u> who was a college wrestler and Big 10 champion named Kevin Wilmot. See top left picture where he is tossing me on my head. From him came many more wrestlers until I had the picture on the right. This picture of the Wheaties box that Cael Sanderson sent to thank me tells a story. What does it say? What doors does this one picture open for me?

My credibility and know-how grew to higher levels and now I can easily interact with world champion level men and women in the wrestling and fight world, or any other sport for that matter.

Now see the bottom left picture of me and Wilmot 19 years later wearing the orange shirts at a recent WINNERS**EDGE** Bootcamp. How cool is it that I was his first chiropractor. Inspired from this <u>he became a chiropractor</u> and is now one of the most solid and successful DCs I know in the world. (This is why I ask him to teach at my Bootcamp.)

If it wasn't for the quality of the adjustments and my dedication to chiropractic, he may have never become a chiropractor, and I would never be connected to the high level fight world today.

<u>You never know what the results from just one adjustment with one patient can bring.</u> <u>We must always be at our best!</u>

Q: Do You Think Advertising Can Still Work for Chiropractors?

Yes, it can work great. From Facebook Ads to events. Print advertising is one of the best and most underutilized marketing out there. The problem is that very few chiropractors can actually create marketing pieces that are good enough to actually spark a response.

The mechanics of mailing are easy. Inserts are easy to do. Door to door is easy to do. Printing is faster and cheaper than ever.

The hard part is writing and making the advertising pieces, the offer, and the pictures good enough to cause people to call.

I would be considered one of the best direct response marketers in chiropractic today. I personally do not know any practicing chiropractor who has generated more chiropractic business as a result of direct response marketing than I have. It may sound like I am bragging but facts are facts. I am highly skilled at this. I can make stuff, mail it, and get the phone to ring. I've paid a ton and have spent many thousands of hours developing this ability over the last 20 years.

The point is, to get someone like me to make even a one page piece for another chiropractor would cost at least $10,000 or more because of the time it takes to create something that will work.

Direct response copyrighting is a career all to itself that requires massive training and experience. Direct response means: *When it hits a person's hands they grab the phone and call.*

So here the doctor sits with direct mail being probably the most underused marketing angle that exists, and almost no way to get their hands on anything good enough to send. The doctor must learn to do it themselves if they want to benefit from it like I have.

To really win you implant a system. You create a great piece to mail to your local homes and businesses then mail 100 every day. Do it every day of every week of every year. I have mailed promotional material every day for over 13 years. I never worried about new patients.

Placemats, magazines, yearbooks, money mailers, water bottles, movie theater ads, ads at the grocery store, ads printed in the local paper, Radio and TV really bring nothing or are too costly to be effective. Some radio can work in certain areas. Direct mail will beat all of them.

"Once a chiropractor reaches 35 patient visits per week they can stop all outside advertising." - Fred Barge DC *Are You The Doctor, Doctor?*

Some say after 100 a week, I personally feel a doctor should crank over 200 then no more outside promo is ever needed again.

Here are a few quick tips for any good marketing piece. This applies to a letter, post card, flyer, mailer, or even emails and online.

All good marketing pieces have:

1. A great **HEADLINE**. This is the bait that gets a reader to look closer. It must enter the conversation in the person's mind.

Sample 1:

We can make your dream practice a reality!

--Or--

Sample 2:

Are You A Chiropractor Who Is Ready To See Another 100 or More Visits Every Week?

How Great Would It Be To Take Home Another $10,000 To $20,000 or More Every Month?

Are You Tired Of Paying On Your Ugly Debt And Finally Want To Learn The Fastest Way To Crush It Once And For All?

Do You Want To Be Personally Taught Exactly How To Get Another 10 To 20 or More New Patients Every Month Without Having To Pay Much To Do It?

2. A great **OFFER** with something people will actually want.

Sample 1:   *Call now for a free consultation!*

-- Or --

Sample 2:   Call today and here is what you will get:

- A **consultation** with the doctor to discuss your health concerns in detail.

- A careful, comfortable, and **complete spinal examination** to discover the underlying cause of your problem.

- If needed, a **complete set of x-rays** will be taken to really see and understand the nature and severity of your problem.

- A **full report** to go over your treatment options and the plan to get you well as fast as possible!

- **And… One complimentary treatment** to show you how gentle and effective our care is.

- You can then decide what is best for you!

- Thousands of people have been helped in our office.

3. A well-presented **DEADLINE** or nothing will happen.

Offer Expires: _April 10th 2019_

4. It must have great **TESTIMONIALS** done properly.

Sample 1:

> *"Dr. Trusty really helped me with my headaches. I can't thank him enough!"* - Jill H

Sample 2:

"After 20+ years in practice, with Dr. Tory and WINNER**SEDGE** I have broken every practice record, my debt is vanishing and I'm saving more $$ than ever! What Tory teaches really is incredible!"
- *Dr. Steve Long – El Dorado Hills, CA*

5. It must have great **copy** to persuade the person and guide them to a decision to call you the expert. *"The more you tell, the more you sell."*

6. Usually a good **map** and great **pictures** strategically taken with the right feeling. People do not look at pictures, they feel pictures.

Sample 1:

Sample 2:

The ability to promote and market yourself, your office, and chiropractic is critical to success. I have endless examples and hours of material on this most important topic. Never make or send anything without these essential elements. Remember: If the promotional piece does not look really good, it is not really good.

Q: Chiropractors Who Want to Grow Usually Hire a Consultant. Do You Have Any Advice for Them?

There are all levels in chiropractic consulting. Bubble gum pep talkers and advice givers, up to the legit big dogs who can handle everything from the simplest question to the most serious, consequential, and complicated patient, business, and practice scenarios.

Does the consultant actually have the ability and means that will cause you to grow in the areas that really matter to you? Or do they just have events and "talk about stuff" with no real plan?

Here are some questions I feel would be incredibly important to ask any potential consultant:

1. **Do you still practice?**

   - Any DC who is out of active practice, real patient, CA, insurance company, and Medicare interaction has "lost it" no matter what they say. They are not even on the playing field with you.

2. **Do you consult out of a living, breathing chiropractic office that I can actually come visit?**

   - Environment is all! Any consultant outside the right environment is at a huge disadvantage. They aren't even in the stadium.

3. **Do you have a training facility where "real life" training and high level events occur?**

   - This is the ultimate. A place to do and see it for real!

4. **Have you, or do you currently own commercial real estate and are a commercial landlord who has written leases?**

   - This is invaluable.

5. **What is your exact plan to get me out of debt?**

   - This is obviously huge.

6. **What is your exact plan to get me to my desired volume level?**

    - This is also huge.

7. **What is your exact plan to get me to become a cash millionaire?**

    - This represents a long-term client goal that most consultants have never even had cross their mind, yet is a most important financial goal. One every chiropractor should absolutely have a plan for.

8. **Have you personally collected, <u>just you alone</u>, from your own efforts, and with no associates or spouses, at least $100,000 in a month from chiropractic? With associates have you collected over $200,000 in a month before?**

    - A person can really only coach to the level they have achieved themselves.

9. **Are you a net worth and cash millionaire yourself from chiropractic and from following your own advice?**

    - You can't hire anyone who is not already what you want to become. (Don't ask for proof as this is going too far. You just want to hear their response.)

10. **What is your contract and what is the early termination fee in case I want to bail early?**

    - You <u>want</u> a contract as it gets the consultant to take you seriously. No contract = no care. Serious contract = serious care.

    - Know the termination fee ahead of time. About 3x the monthly fee is fair. I have chiros right now who can't join my group because they are stuck in evil and abusive termination clauses with other groups who did nothing for them. One is stuck paying $9000. What a joke.

    - Remember you want to hire a <u>consultant</u>. <u>One primary expert to guide you</u>. Avoid joining some nebulous "group" in hopes that someone in it may be able to help you find success. <u>Get a real expert who is directly committed to you</u> via an agreement.

11. **How many online videos do you have for instant application?**

    - To give you an idea, we have 500 and growing.

12. **How many events do you have every year and what is their purpose?**

    - To compare: We have 13 events: 5 main Seminars, 4 Trainings, 2 DC Bootcamps, 2 major CA Trainings, and now have the Team Bootcamp and Money Bootcamp emerging. 8 are held in the incredible WINNERSEDGE Training Center.

13. **What all do you have for CA and Team Training?**

14. **What is your goal for me in the first 90 days with you?**

15. **Do I get a private call, a group call or no set call?**

    - The consistent private call with the expert is the best. Group calls or "call when you want" is pretty weak.

16. **What is the physical condition of the consultant? Hire a consultant who is clearly the real thing. A physical and mental specimen.**

17. **If it matters to you, what is the consultant's world view?**

    - Doctors ask all the time if I am a Christian for example.

18. **What have you published for CD sets, DVD sets, books or other products that will help me grow faster?**

    - For comparison: I am at 32 CD/DVD sets, 4 books, 3 booklets, plus the library of over 500 videos.

19. **What do you see as the three most important things, systems, procedures or disciplines I have to have in place in order to grow?**

20. **Do you personally care about my growth? Do you take it personally or do you really not care whether I grow or not? Do you see my success as your success? Do you take me, my practice, and my future seriously?**

I could not help but add a few bits of my own information. As you can tell, we feel we're on top of our game. Nobody out there does what we do at the level we do it.

But... every DC must find who they feel most comfortable with.

It is not so much about the cost. It is about what you get. One group could cost $800 per month and your NET PROFIT doesn't even grow $2000 per month.

Another group could have a fee of $1500 per month but you learn how to save $50,000 on your student loan interest, you learn how to help another 100 patients every week, you collect $15,000 more every month, and you are inspired to workout more. Who was "cheaper?"

So the final questions are: *"What exactly do I get for my money if I decide to join your group?* And *"Explain to me exactly how can I get at least 5 to 100x a return on my money?"*

Q: What Are Some of The Biggest Mistakes You See Chiropractors Make?

A lot of these are already in this booklet somewhere. I will just do a Top 10 list.

Tory's Top 10 DC mistakes in no particular order:

1. No coach, or quit coaching at a low level for a lame reason.

2. No money disciplines, no good money system in place.

3. Wrong floorplan and office layout.

4. No scripted Report, Re-sign system, and Wellness plans in place.

5. No or weak Team Meeting.

6. Doctor is dressed wrong and so is staff.

7. Lack of fearlessness in promoting.

8. Lack of technique, hands-on skill, and tableside manner.

9. Doctor is not "into" their own health and fitness.

10. A Chiropractic Philosophy tank that is bone dry.

Q: Is There a Difference Between How the Less Successful Chiropractors Talk Compared to How the More Successful Chiropractors Talk?

Great question. You can tell a lot by the words a person uses in day to day conversation. It tells you how they really think. Earl Nightingale taught us years ago: *"We become what we think about."*

Now do this. Read both of the following lists and notice how they each feel. Notice how the first list of phrases makes you feel. Then compare it to how you feel after reading the second "successful" set of phrases.

Here are some things that the less successful or "off mission" chiropractor says:

- I just put everything on credit cards, it's a lot easier.

- I pay too much in taxes, how can I cut them?

- How do I lower my overhead?

- I really don't have much to save right now. I'll get to it later.

- I learned a new investment; I am going to be my own bank!

- Hey, I'm adding these "great" multilevel products to my office, you should really check it out.

- That is expensive.

- I can't afford that.

- I'm having a down week.

- My numbers are down.

- How much does it cost?

- I want people to judge me for who I am and not how I look.

- How do I combat the insurance companies who cut my bill?
- I don't need any technique seminars, I have it down.
- Hold on, I need to get my spouse on the phone with me.
- Hold on, my CA is going to join us on the call.
- Once I have more money then I will start saving.
- Once I am in a little better shape then I will start working out.
- Once I get more new ones coming in I will do more marketing.
- I will start giving money away once I have more of it.
- Why would I give money away, someone should give me some money.
- I'm not sure how much of my student loan payment is going to interest. I never really look at it.
- I am going to buy a house right away. I'm not going to throw away any money on rent.
- I don't know anything about taxes, I just have my tax lady do it all at the end of the year.
- How do I get more new ones?
- Why can't I keep any good CAs?
- I'm overwhelmed right now and I'm not sure what to do.
- I'm off to a bad start this week.
- I need to do some advertising.
- I can't afford the Bootcamp.
- I will start referring once somebody refers to me first.
- Philosophy books? Like what do you mean?
- I'm doing everything but nobody is coming in.
- I can afford the payments, so it's all good.
- I don't feel comfortable telling people about what I do.
- I'm thinking of adding an associate so I can take more time off.

- My house is my best asset.
- I don't have time to work out.
- No, I won't be at the seminar.
- My CA doesn't want to go to any seminars or trainings.
- I don't like to read that much.
- I need new patients.
- I need money.

I'm just going to stop there because these are depressing. Negative thoughts come from a negative mind. Positive thoughts come from a positive mind. *A positive mind attracts positive results!*

Now read this list of how successful chiropractors talk. Tell me how these statements make you feel:

- I'll pay cash.
- Taxes are just part of business, so I pay them first.
- How do I increase my profit?
- I started saving with just $10 per week because I knew I had to create the habit. I will increase it over time.
- I'm not going to waste time on anything outside my profession. *Jack of all trades = master of none.*
- What is it worth?
- I can't afford that just yet, but I will soon.
- It can be done.
- I will catch them, because I always do.
- It's the calm before the storm. We have lots of room for great new and returning patients this week!
- I love who I see in the book, and there's lots of room for more.
- I'm not so concerned about the cost. I want to know what it is worth first.

- I know my image is everything. I always look right.
- Great, I can convert the patients to cash now.
- I love technique and try to get 1 or 2 seminars in every year.
- I will handle this, I don't need anyone's approval.
- I have my marketing system in place. It's really great.
- The harder I work the luckier I get.
- I give money away, especially when I am lean. I know I've got to give first in order to receive later.
- All the new patients I require to reach my goals are on their way to me right now.
- I always get good CAs. They are a reflection of me.
- I attract what I am.
- Alcohol on a night before work, are you kidding me?
- I will figure it out.
- I will get it done.
- My practice is my best asset so I take great care of it!
- I love being a chiropractor.
- I am on a mission!
- How can I better my treatment time by another 15 seconds?
- Of course I have a perfectly scripted and memorized report.
- I talk to my coach every week, of course.
- I talk to my accountant every couple weeks or so.
- I am a physical and mental chiropractic success machine.
- I am a chiropractic powerhouse.
- Yeah my website is about as good as we can possibly get it. I am especially happy with the videos I made for it.
- With chiropractic principles on my side I always succeed.
- There is always a way to win, and I will find it.

- People love referring new patients to me.
- I just finished reading this great book.
- At my workout today I did...
- Of course my team and I will be at the seminar.
- Sign me up for the next Bootcamp.
- I LOVE new patients.
- I LOVE and appreciate money.

Notice how great you feel after reading these positive statements! I have countless more memorized. We have entire CDs with nothing but chiropractic success affirmations. They work!

It is very important that we be constantly re-programming our minds for success. There is so much negative out there that we must counter it with successful, positive, inspiring words and images.

Another important tool is asking great questions. If you can learn to ask yourself smart questions you will be amazed at what happens in your life.

When you ask yourself a question, your subconscious mind goes to work to find the solution for you. It is a secret weapon of the super achiever. They know if they pose a question to their subconscious mind, it has the ability to direct you to whatever may be required for it to be answered or made real.

Here are a few smart questions a chiropractor might ask:

➢ How can I grow 100 visits a week in under 90 days?

➢ How can I pay my student loans off by the end of next year?

➢ How can I be a better adjuster and draw more referrals?

➢ How can I dress better and look more credible?

➢ How can I have the perfect office for less rent?

➢ How can I get a banner in the local gym?

➢ How can I save one million dollars in under 10 years?

> How can I get every patient to refer at least one person?

> How can I get my treatment time down by 15 seconds?

> How can I attract the best CA for my office?

> How can I work out at least 3 days a week and never miss?

> How can I increase my visits per week and refine my hours at the same time?

> What do I need to do to get more Attorneys to refer to me?

> Where is the best location for my new office?

> How can I have my practice completely paid off by the end of the year?

What is something you want? Put it in the form of a question and speak it out loud sincerely. Ask any question you like. Be bold!

"The quality of your life is dependent upon the quality of the questions you ask yourself." - Demartini

Q: Did You Have Any Money Guidelines for Chiropractors to See If They Are on Track or Behind Financially?

Yes, we talked about it a little earlier. I can also simplify it down like this. There can be some variation of course.

After 5 years in practice: $50,000 saved and crushing debt.

After 10 years: $200,000 saved and student loans paid in full.

After 15 years: $500,000 saved and NO debt other than a mortgage.

After 20 years: $750,000 saved and full acceleration on mortgage.

After 25 years: $1,000,000 saved and home completely paid.

After 30 years: $1,500,000 saved and no debt.

Q: Tory, This Is Really Great Stuff. Did You Want to Try and Summarize This All for Us?

Sure, I think I've given a lot of valuable nuggets on a variety of things. I want to be sure we are focused and leave knowing what the main goal is and how to get there.

The main purpose of this booklet is to teach the importance of smart money handling and to introduce a better money flow system into the chiropractor's life. Just know it will cause your practice to grow.

The goal is to be such a good chiropractor that tons of people come see you. You get great results and collect a significant amount of money. Once the money hits your hands you then handle it well.

WINNERSEDGE Money Flow steps summarized.

I've numbered them below. Get them all implemented as fast as you can even if you have to go out of order.

Step 1: Get all your file folders, online banking, and accounts perfectly labeled and organized. No winging it ever again.

Step 2: Do: **Dr. Robson's** *Practice Growth and Money Flow Bootcamp* videos and financial worksheets. For WINNERSEDGE members. Fax to me so I can go over them with you.

Step 3: Get an accountant who can do all your books, taxes <u>and</u> your payroll automatically like we teach. I've never touched QuickBooks or done my own payroll. Why would I?

Step 4: Pay yourself weekly an amount you can afford, or enough to cover your personal expenses.

Step 5: As you get paid every week, also pay your federal and any state tax deposits automatically of an estimated amount based on your projected collections.

Step 6: If you owe back taxes get a payment arrangement made to handle them as fast as possible. There is no excuse for owing back taxes of any kind EVER again.

Step 7: Set up your *Rapid Fire.* Make the minimum payment on all debts. Pick the smallest one and hammer it with additional automated weekly payments and or daily payments.

Step 8: Get car payments going weekly of an amount that adds up to more than the regular monthly payment, so it pays off faster.

Step 9: Set up a Money Market savings account and start automatically saving a comfortable amount weekly recurring forever. Start with $10 per week if you have to. <u>The goal is to get the SYSTEM in place.</u> You can raise the amounts later. You can save automatically from the business account into one savings account. In addition, you can save automatically from your personal checking account into a different savings account. I call this the *Double Vortex Accelerated Saving System*.

Step 10: Pay staff every two weeks. Make their automated federal and any state payroll tax deposits just like you do yourself. The accountant should be able to handle all this for you.

Step 11: Find a cause or charity you want to donate to, something that matters to you. Set them up in your online Bill Pay and send them money every month automatically. Again, start with $20 per month if that is all you can swing for now. Believe me, the need is great. They will be grateful for it.

Understand when your collections go up you owe more tax <u>right now</u>. You must see this. <u>NEVER wait for an accountant to tell you anything. Your money is your business. You are 100% responsible</u> to be on top of your game.

Keep diligent track of all statements in organized folders in a cabinet and online. Be super organized at all times.

Save copies of everything forever. I have every year's tax return in a cabinet. Yes, all 20 years.

Make it your mission to become a money handling expert. Be a person who can hold on to money. Be a person who can grow money. Be a person who is super reliable with money. It will change your entire life. You will inspire others and be living proof that it can be done.

Q: Any Final Thoughts?

You bet. Keep it simple, stay focused, always have written down goals, and work hard until you have what you want.

A chiropractor is a unique person. We have to wear all the hats. We are the one who hires, trains, fires, markets, pays bills, collects, treats, and the other 1000 responsibilities in and out of the office.

Any man or woman who accepts this challenge is worthy of incredible respect. They deserve to be rewarded with an incredible life filled with love, happiness, and success.

So:

1. Get the **WE money system** in place.
2. Have a perfectly memorized **Report** script.
3. **Save** your age. **Crush debt** to stop the financial bleeding.
4. Get in **great physical condition** and never get lazy on this.
5. **Get a coach** and pay the price it takes to have a great life.
6. **No big houses** until debt is gone and you can afford it.
7. Be **giving money away** even if times are real lean.
8. Remember and use our **Doberman Philosophy.**
9. **God is in control** and His plans will ultimately prevail.
10. **Chill**, in 75 years none of what worries you will matter anyway.

So you might as well just go for it!

Thanks a Ton Tory! This Material Is Life Changing.

Thank you. I hope it has value for all who read it.

Q: Tory, What Other Materials Do You Have for Us?

I have all these CD and DVD Sets available on my website.

Large Sets:

CA Training Mastery *10 Disc Set*

Communication and Persuasion System *9 Disc Set*

Build a Huge Personal Injury Practice *10 Disc Set*

The New Patient Generator *4 Disc and Template Set*

Office Forms *Complete set all in Microsoft Word Format*

Office Visit Talk *13 Disc Set*

Overhead and Practice Money Mastery *8 Disc Set*

Practice Promotion Mastery *12 Disc Set*

Technique Mastery *12 Disc Set*

Small Sets

Treatment Time Mastery *4 Disc Set plus Materials*

Become a New Patient Magnet *4 Disc Set*

Become a Re-Sign Master *2 Disc Set*

Chiro Prosperity Secrets *4 Disc Set*

Chiro Start Up Essentials *4 Disc Set*

Double Your Patient Referrals *2 Disc Set*

Double Your PVA *4 Disc Set*

Pro CA Essentials *2 Disc Set*

Pro Chiro Talk *2 Disc Set*

Pro Chiro Talk II *2 Disc Set*

Promo and Marketing that Actually Works for DCs *2 Disc Set*

Prosperity Affirmations for Chiropractors *2 Disc Set*

Recharging Your Practice *2 Disc Set*

Report Mastery *4 Disc Set*

Save Money, Crush Debt, be Financially Free *4 Disc Set*

The 5 Plays *4 Disc Set*

The 20 To Dos for Chiro Super Success *2 Disc Set*

The Million Dollar Practice *4 Disc Set*

Live and Inspired *Convicting Health Talk recorded live 2 DVDs*

<u>**For DCs and Non DCs**</u>

7 Pillars of Personal and Professional Success *16 Disc + Workbook Set*

The Image Doctor *180 page Hardcover Book by Dr. Robson*

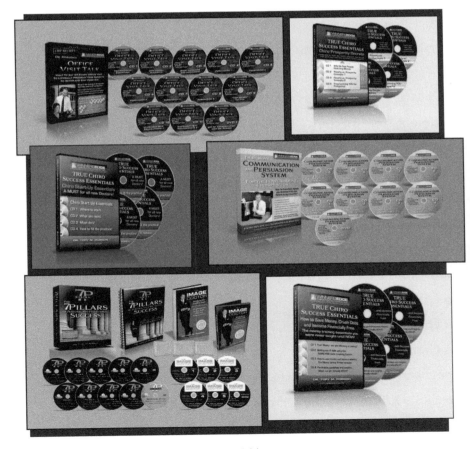

Q: Now a Little More About Your Coaching Program?

We have many information delivery elements:

Calls

- I do a one-hour video *Zoom* call <u>every week</u>. All member DCs can be on. These are incredible. And all are recorded.
- You can also choose to have private scheduled training call with me directly.
- CAs also have a one-hour video *Zoom* call with me and any featured CAs every month. Our CA Training is excellent.
- All member DCs and CAs can call or <u>email me directly</u> anytime with practice questions. My accessibility is what makes us unique.

Website

- You get passcodes to our 500+ practice success videos in our amazing **Video Library**. One of our many secret weapons.
- Here you can download our incredible 12 Phase **Practice Transformation Guide**. It works, believe me!
- You can also access all recorded and archived *Zoom* training calls.
- All Seminars are made into a 30-min synopsis video including our Seminar Booklet for those unable to attend.
- You get our invaluable list of WINNERSEDGE resources and contacts. Websites, equipment, experts, marketing, everything.
- All our products can be purchased on our website, many with Members Only pricing.

Events

- 5 **True Chiro Success Seminars** each year for all DCs, spouses and staff. All member DCs have a nametag waiting for them.
- Access to all **Workshops**, and our legendary DC and CA **Bootcamps**.
- I also offer private trainings in your office or in my own office!

And

- WINNERSEDGE Toolkit: Practice, Business and CA Essentials plus Bonus materials are sent to all members ASAP.
- All members get my direct email!
- CAs also have access to all things WINNERSEDGE!

At **WINNERSEDGE** we basically have three programs. But I have been known to make custom programs for DCs in unique situations or locations, like Mexico City, Jakarta or Singapore for example.

We are ready for DCs **starting** or buying a practice, **new** DCs in their first 2 years open, and **established** DCs who've been running for over 2 years.

$Mach1^x$ **This is our Exclusive high-end program.**

- Perfect for Multi-DC, Multi-location clinics and for *On-Fire* DCs who want to grow as fast as possible.
- DCs get a <u>weekly</u> private training call from me directly.
- Plus they get my personal cell phone number for text coaching.
- This is for DCs who want the ultimate in private consulting.

Mach1 **Our signature program that nearly all DCs do.**

- DCs get a monthly private call from me.

Cruiser **For successful DCs to stay sharp after success in *Mach1***

- This program is for our members who have been *Mach1* for years and have all systems and money flow well in order. Members can attend events, call or email on their own.

I feel that nobody in chiropractic has a training program as complete, intense and fun as we have right now. We are on top of our game and will be for many years.

WHAT IS SUCCESS? TO LAUGH OFTEN AND MUCH; TO WIN THE RESPECT OF INTELLIGENT PEOPLE AND THE AFFECTION OF CHILDREN; TO EARN THE APPRECIATION OF HONEST CRITICS AND ENDURE THE BETRAYAL OF FALSE FRIENDS; TO APPRECIATE BEAUTY; TO FIND THE BEST IN OTHERS; TO LEAVE THE WORLD A BIT BETTER, WHETHER BY A HEALTHY CHILD, A GARDEN PATCH OR A REDEEMED SOCIAL CONDITION; TO KNOW EVEN ONE LIFE HAS BREATHED EASIER BECAUSE YOU HAVE LIVED; THAT IS TO HAVE SUCCEEDED.

-RALPH WALDO EMERSON

For DCs willing to do what it takes to be the best.